Teaching and Learning
in the Face of Adversity

Teaching and Learning in the Face of Adversity

Strategies That Inspire

Michelle L. Trujillo
Center for Learning and Well-Being

Douglas Fisher
San Diego State University

Nancy Frey
San Diego State University

CORWIN
A Sage Company

A Sage Company

FOR INFORMATION:

Corwin

A Sage Company

2455 Teller Road

Thousand Oaks, California 91320

(800) 233-9936

www.corwin.com

Sage Publications Ltd.

1 Oliver's Yard

55 City Road

London EC1Y 1SP

United Kingdom

Sage Publications India Pvt. Ltd.

Unit No 323-333, Third Floor, F-Block

International Trade Tower Nehru Place

New Delhi 110 019

India

Sage Publications Asia-Pacific Pte. Ltd.

18 Cross Street #10-10/11/12

China Square Central

Singapore 048423

Vice President and Editorial
  Director: Monica Eckman

Publisher: Jessica Allan

Senior Content Development
  Editor: Mia Rodriguez

Senior Editorial Assistant: Natalie Delpino

Production Editor: Laura Barrett

Copy Editor: Amy Hanquist Harris

Typesetter: C&M Digitals (P) Ltd.

Proofreader: Theresa Kay

Cover Designer: Candice Harman

Marketing Manager: Olivia Barlett

Library of Congress Control Number: 2024942996

This book is printed on acid-free paper.

24 25 26 27 28 10 9 8 7 6 5 4 3 2 1

DISCLAIMER: This book may direct you to access third-party content via web links, QR codes, or other scannable technologies, which are provided for your reference by the author(s). Corwin makes no guarantee that such third-party content will be available for your use and encourages you to review the terms and conditions of such third-party content. Corwin takes no responsibility and assumes no liability for your use of any third-party content, nor does Corwin approve, sponsor, endorse, verify, or certify such third-party content.

CONTENTS

ABOUT THE AUTHORS

Michelle Trujillo is Co-Founder of the Center for Learning and Well-Being and is passionate about igniting hope in schools and the workplace! A lifelong educator, Michelle is known to make a tangible, sustainable, and positive difference through her books, keynotes, and interactive workshops. Named Nevada's 2016 Innovative Educator of the Year, Michelle has appeared on television (including *Oprah*), podcasts, and radio stations across the nation. Michelle partners with school districts, professional educational associations, educational service agencies, and conference organizers to provide applicable and inspiring strategies in the realm of school culture and climate, social emotional learning, and restorative practice. A bestselling author, Michelle's books include: *Social Emotional Well-Being for Educators, Start with the Heart: Igniting Hope in Schools Through Social and Emotional Learning* and *Chicken Soup for the Soul Presents Teens Talkin' Faith*.

Douglas Fisher is professor and chair of educational leadership at San Diego State University and a leader at Health Sciences High and Middle College. Previously, Doug was an early intervention teacher and elementary school educator. He is a credentialed teacher and leader in California. In 2022, he was inducted into the Reading Hall of Fame by the Literacy Research Association. He has published widely on literacy, quality instruction, and assessment, as well as books such as *Welcome to Teaching*, *PLC+*, *Teaching Students to Drive Their Learning*, and *Student Assessment: Better Evidence, Better Decisions, Better Learning.*

Nancy Frey is professor of educational leadership at San Diego State University and a leader at Health Sciences High and Middle College. Previously, Nancy was a teacher, academic coach, and central office resource coordinator in Florida. She is a credentialed special educator, reading specialist, and administrator in

California. She is a member of the International Literacy Association's Literacy Research Panel. She has published widely on literacy, quality instruction, and assessment, as well as books such as *The Artificial Intelligence Playbook, How Scaffolding Works, How Teams Work,* and *The Vocabulary Playbook*.

INTRODUCTION

Adversity is all around us. It is central to the human experience to encounter challenges and barriers in our daily lives. Some of these challenges are relatively minor; others are significant, life-changing events. This book is not about changing the fact that educators, students, and families encounter adversity; rather, it is about our ability as educators to empower ourselves, our colleagues, and our students to elevate the way in which we respond to adversity.

Truth be told, we might wish these adversities away, and it would be great to have fewer challenges in our lives. But we are reminded of Maya Angelou's advice: "You may encounter many defeats, but you must not be defeated. In fact, it may be necessary to encounter the defeats so you can know who you are, what you can rise from, how you can still come out of it."

It seems that some amount of adversity is helpful and allows us to grow and develop. After all, as we may have heard, "adversity is one of life's great teachers." Be assured, we are not suggesting that educators or students simply accept the range of adversities in their lives and suffer. When taken too far, resilience "may focus individuals on impossible goals and make them unnecessarily tolerant of unpleasant or counterproductive circumstances" (Chamorro-Premuzic & Lusk, 2017, para. 10).

Instead, this book is realistic and applicable. It addresses the ways in which we respond to the range of challenges—adversities—that arise as we do our work. There are healthy and not-so-healthy ways to respond to these events and situations. And there are skills we can develop and help our students to cultivate to elevate our ability to respond to adversity. We can reduce the negative impact of these adversities as well as enhance our learning and create opportunities from the challenges, obstacles, or even traumatic experiences we face.

In fact, there is a proficiency range when it comes to addressing adversity. Humans have a wide range of intelligences, and these develop with experience and learning. We are not talking about the multiple intelligences movement, which mistakenly suggested that learning experiences should align with one type of intelligence such as linguistic or musical. Rather, we are thinking about quotients that represent different clusters of behavior that can be learned. In a *Forbes* magazine article, Dennison (2022) notes that there are several different quotients that can be considered:

- **Intelligence Quotient (IQ):** The ability to recognize and solve problems
- **Emotional Quotient (EQ):** Measures emotional intelligence, self-awareness, and emotional self-control
- **Adversity Quotient (AQ):** The ability to face and overcome adverse situations
- **Social Quotient (SQ):** Determines cultural fit and social awareness
- **Cognitive Quotient (CQ):** How one utilizes their intelligence

Importantly, these are demonstrated in the ways humans display behavior, their communication styles, the talents they cultivate, and how they approach projects and problems. The word choice *quotient* is important, as it means the degree or amount of some characteristic. In other words, at a given time an individual may have more or less of one of these characteristics. And these are influenced by culture, experiences, and opportunities.

Unfortunately, these models can be misused. For example, in history there was a mistaken belief that intelligence could be easily measured using a test and the scores used to label and sort people (e.g., Terman, 1916). In fact, some experts believed that the results of these tests could be used to predict the future success of the individual, and thus classes were organized for children based on their scores on these assessments.

Having said that, psychologists still recognize that humans have intelligence and have attempted to quantify it, now recognizing that scores on these types of assessments reflect the experiences that the learner has had rather than their future success. We also recognize that "thinking should be measured by an intelligence test and knowing by an achievement test" (Naglieri, 2020). Further, it's important to separate the concept of intelligence from other areas of human development.

We introduce the idea of various quotients to underscore the fact that these are not fixed areas of performance, but rather continue to grow and develop across our lifetimes. In this book, our focus is on adversity and the ways in which we can elevate our own adversity quotient and that of our students. It concerns a collection of behaviors that allow us to respond when we encounter barriers, frustrations, setbacks, and unpleasant events in our lives.

As Stoltz (1997) proposed, the adversity quotient is a person's ability to face situations, problems, and obstacles in life and contains four components: control, ownership, reach, and endurance (see Figure i.1).

i.1 Components of the Adversity Quotient

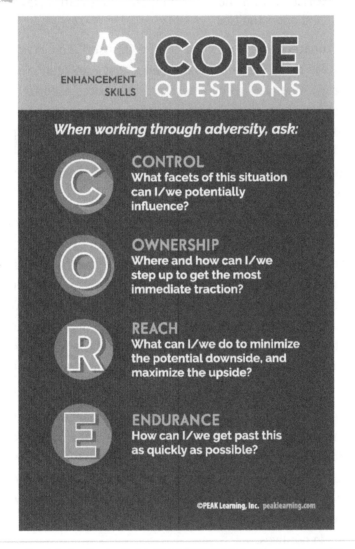

Source: Reprinted with permission from PEAK Learning, Inc. PEAK Learning Inc. are the creators and owners of the AQ® theory, assessment, and method as well as CORE®. Visit www.peaklearning.com for more information.

- **Control** is our ability to take command of situations and our responses to those situations. We recognize what we can control in a situation rather than becoming overwhelmed by things that are beyond our control.

- **Ownership** is our ability to take responsibility for our responses and actions. It requires that we avoid blaming others or outside factors for the challenges. Instead, we focus on the steps we can take to improve the situations, resulting in greater self-efficacy and the recognition that our efforts and the outcomes are connected.

- **Reach** is our ability to respond to adverse situations and to seek help and support when needed. We build a network of supportive relationships and resources to reduce the feelings of isolation or we find support and guidance to help us overcome challenges.

- **Endurance** is our ability to persist through difficult times and face challenges. This helps us rebound from problems and maintain a positive attitude even when circumstances are trying. This strength helps us reach our goals.

The question we have asked often over the last several years is, "What does it take to elevate one's adversity quotient?"—and by adversity quotient, we mean one's ability to persevere in the face of significant adversity. Throughout our combined years in education, we've interacted with many educators, students, and families who have thrived in the midst of adversity, while others have been easily overcome by challenging situations, leading to a sense of helplessness and hopelessness. In this case, those who fail or struggle to thrive would typically have a lower adversity quotient. Essentially, they lack hope, and thus are less inspired or able to confront or conquer potential trials or tribulations. It is our premise that tangible hope can kick-start one's ability to persevere.

The term *tangible* is intentional. Like toxic positivity, hope without action is ineffective. Tangible hope, however, is concrete, substantial, and subsequently transformative. Cornel West (Samuel, 2020) suggested, "Hope is not only a virtue; it is also a verb." Hope can play a vital role in developing and cultivating one's capacity to adapt and persist through adversity. Moreover, as a verb, "hope" transcends an expectation or desire for a specific action to occur and serves as a motivational impetus for attaining a goal, striving for growth, or finding purpose in life and in learning. In fact, according to a revealing study, *hope*, defined as a "multidimensional positive motivational state," can impact academic functioning and student well-being. Within their study, Bryce et al. (2019) suggest that "cognitive hope, which encompasses motivation and approach to goal attainment, and behavioral hope, which includes regulation for goal attainment, both play critical roles in promoting youths' academic functioning and life outcomes."

This applicable concept of hope is also reflected in the title of an article in the *Journal of Research in Personality*: "Hope uniquely predicts objective academic achievement above intelligence, personality, and previous academic achievement" (Day et al., 2010). Furthermore, scientists have discovered that not only does hope reside in the medial orbital frontal cortex of the brain, but as a result, it can act to mediate anxiety by increasing endorphins (Ratner, 2019). We know that when students feel anxious or stressed, their ability to learn can be inhibited. As educators, we ignite hope in the lives of our students when we create the valuable pedagogical link that connects ongoing meaningful instruction and engaged learning to desired life outcomes. We understand that hope must be tangible and requires that we have goals and develop agency, self-efficacy, and resiliency. As such, hope is inexplicably connected to elevating one's adversity quotient.

Stoltz has developed an Adversity Quotient assessment to help people understand how they respond to adversity and thus help people increase the ability to handle difficulties.

It's focused more on business, but you can get a sense of the types of questions that are used to identify each of the four components of your adversity quotient (https://smallbusi nessmattersonline.com/wp-content/uploads/2013/07/The-Adversity-Quotient.pdf).

WHAT IS THE PURPOSE OF THIS BOOK?

Every one of the adults who functions as an educator faces adversity, as does every student. Consider the prayer for serenity by Reinhold Niebuhr: *God, grant me the serenity to accept the things I cannot change, the courage to change the things I can, and the wisdom to know the difference.*

Thus, the goals of this book:

- To help you understand and accept things you cannot change, but to do so in ways that nourish your well-being and that of your students.

- To provide awareness of thoughts, words, and behaviors within your sphere of influence and sphere of concern so you do not waste time focused on situations beyond your control.

- To develop skills in the way you respond to adverse experiences, including courage to change situations and understand your role in that change.

- To empower you with strategies to foster your students' abilities to effectively respond to adversity.

With these goals in mind, we aim to remind you through the content of this book that, as educators, we are ignitors of hope! Our students, our students' families, and our colleagues need us to serve in this role now, more than ever before. Therefore, it is imperative that we face our trials, both those we've come to expect and those that appear out of nowhere and shake us to our core, with *hope*. As such, we will pursue our goals for this book through the lens of igniting hope.

We will share ideas, anecdotes, and strategies that are within your realm of control, will nourish your well-being, engage your students, and foster positive and productive relationships.

Furthermore, know that we believe in the concept of *all teach, all learn*. Regardless of the role we serve within our school community—teacher, paraprofessional, school counselor, educational leader, bus driver, or any other role—we all have lessons to teach, and we all have something to learn, especially in the face of adversity. Consider, too, that our student learners can be our best teachers.

Finally, the contents of this book are timeless and meant to meet educators in the moment, especially in the midst of challenges or uncertainty. Global pandemics may occur once in a lifetime, challenging educational mandates may come and go, but adversity is a genuine and consistent experience—a certain companion in life. Former First Lady Michelle Obama (2011) shared this wisdom at a keynote address in South Africa: "You may not always have a comfortable life, and you will not always be able to solve all of the world's problems at once, but don't ever underestimate the importance you can have because history has shown us that courage can be contagious, and hope can take on a life of its own."

As you embark on the journey that is this book, we invite you, as our readers and fellow educators, to participate—to read, learn, reflect, and share. In doing so, we are confident you will gain the awareness, knowledge, and skills to ignite hope, nourish well-being, and engage students in a quest to elevate your adversity quotient and that of your students!

1

BE INTENTIONAL

When you're intentional, you can add value to
everything you do and to every person you meet.

—John C. Maxwell

In the Introduction, we suggested that adversity is ever-present and life's certain companion. What we didn't address is the reality, which we have all experienced, that some of the adversity we face in life is completely out of our control, while other challenges or obstacles are of our own making. So we begin our exploration of elevating one's ability to respond to adversity by focusing on the skill of being intentional. In fact, we ignite hope in the lives of others when we choose to be intentional. Additionally, a focus on intentionality can create responses from others that will cause us to feel more hopeful ourselves. More importantly, being intentional fosters behaviors that help us and others to encounter difficulties with courage, while nourishing one's well-being.

This lesson, like the three that follow, is organized into three sections. First, we present an opportunity to increase our awareness of the application of hope in the face of adversity.

For example, in Lesson One we explore the way in which *being intentional* can ignite hope by expanding our awareness as well as our ability to identify circumstances that are within our realm of control so that our response helps rather than hinders a situation.

Next, we provide a section focused on choices that nourish one's well-being. Within this section, we ask you to identify adverse experiences that are out of your sphere of influence and provide strategies for cultivating courage to evidence impact through changing that which is within your control. Our intention is to propose ideas and strategies that nurture one's well-being through thoughts, words, and behaviors that are inherent to our daily routines and vital to education.

Finally, the third section is designed with purpose to promote opportunities to foster student agency, self-efficacy, and engagement in the midst of adversity.

 PROMPTS TO PONDER

- What is one word that comes to mind when you consider what it means to be intentional?
- How might being intentional impact your well-being or that of your students when challenging situations, personal hardships, or professional frustrations occur?
- How might focusing on intentionality improve your instructional practice?
- How might student engagement and achievement be affected by educators being more intentional in their thoughts, words, and actions?

IGNITE!

To be intentional means to think before we act, making choices with consideration of the impact on ourselves and others. Nearly 50 percent of people live their lives on autopilot, going through the motions while our minds wander. Not surprisingly, doing so makes us unhappy (Killingsworth & Gilbert, 2010). Conversely, choosing to be intentional can infuse significance and value into our every thought, word, action, or behavior. For example, being intentional about "why" we do what we do can bring meaning and purpose into our work, grounding us in our passion and helping us to remain motivated and committed when we encounter adversity. In fact, when we become disconnected from why we originally chose our vocation, we inadvertently allow frustration and disillusionment to seep into our daily routine and disrupt our ability to persevere.

We encourage you to intentionally identify your *why* and keep it in your hearts and at the forefront of all you do every day. In fact, take a moment to consider your why. Was there a person, experience, value, or passion in your life that influenced your decision to choose your vocation? Some of us can bring our reason immediately to mind. Others of us may need time to marinate or think intentionally about why we chose a human-oriented profession. Which one are you? If you are one who can identify your why easily, take time to share in the following space. If, on the other hand, you need more time to reflect, please come back in the next day or two and share your thoughts.

_____

_____

_____

_____

_____

_____

_____

_____

_____

There are two primary reasons for identifying and reflecting on our why. First, so often in the typical world of education we can get lost in the essential yet potentially overwhelming responsibility of accelerating student learning, implementing initiatives, measuring outcomes, using data to drive instruction, and creating school culture. Add the reality of the protocols, procedures, requirements, and trainings that must be in place for us to even consider best instructional practices, and it is understandable that over the last few years we may have lost sight of our why. However, we cannot let our known responsibilities or inconceivable unforeseen challenges distract us from that which is right in front of us: the human beings whom we teach and lead and those with whom we serve. When we stay connected to our why, people remain our focus, and we realize that so many little things really do matter! A smile in the hallway or the use of one's name during a class session ignites hope for a positive day, a word of encouragement or an opportunity provided for students to work together to seek solutions ignites hope for learning, and setting a high expectation ignites hope that personal and academic success is attainable.

The second reason we encourage you to be intentional in identifying your why is that when we know why we do what we do, we are able to set relevant and meaningful goals as we tackle adversity. In fact, establishing short- and long-term goals helps people operationalize their why. These goals serve as mile markers in our quests to live our why. We're not talking about to-do lists, but rather goals that allow you to work toward your vision. Goals should be specific and difficult. Locke and

Latham (1991) note there are five goal-setting principles that can help improve your chances of success:

1. *Clarity.* Setting goals that are clear and specific allows people to track progress and reduces the confusion that can arise when goals are not clear.

2. *Challenging.* Accomplishing difficult goals builds our efficacy and the belief that we can do hard things. As we experience success, we create a winning mindset that builds our adversity quotient.

3. *Commitment.* Clear and challenging goals require that we commit to take action to accomplish the goal.

4. *Feedback.* Seeking feedback and acting on that feedback allows us to adjust our expectations and our plan of action going forward.

5. *Task complexity.* The goal should allow for clear steps or actions, and these should be sufficiently complex to ensure that the goal is met.

Later in this chapter, we will focus on goal setting. The goals you set to build your adversity quotient should align with your why. Consider each of these questions about the goals that you set and identify an accountability partner who can provide you feedback.

➤ What is a school-related or personal goal you have for yourself?

➤ How does this connect with your why?

➤ What has your past performance been like? What has been your personal best so far?

➤ How will achieving this goal benefit you?

➤ How will you know you have been successful?

➤ What might get in the way of you meeting this goal?

➤ What resources do you need to achieve this goal?

Another intentional choice that won't add to our busy schedules is simply changing the way in which we look at things. Some may call this a mindset shift; the research world calls it cognitive reframing (Pipas & Pepper, 2021). We can choose to see people and situations through the lens of deficits, or we can choose to reframe our thinking or words in order to see or express what might be possible in any given situation. For example, a teacher who has a student in class who is consistently disruptive can choose to see that student as disrespectful and unruly or as a student who embodies perseverance. If the teacher chooses the latter perspective, then an opportunity exists to encourage the student to use this character trait to engage in class in a more positive way. Of course, the disruptive behavior needs to stop, but how we frame the situation impacts our well-being.

We have discussed being intentional in our mindset, as well as some of our specific choices in the context of words or actions. The choice to *believe* intentionally—in our students, our colleagues, and ourselves—fosters our ability to ignite hope and is worthy of a deeper dive. Collective teacher efficacy has a positive influence on student learning (Goddard et al., 2004). Collective teacher (or educator, to be more inclusive) efficacy can be defined as the *belief* that we, as a group of educators, have in our students' ability to achieve *and* the belief that we have in our own ability, as a group, to make an impact on their learning. In essence, we must believe together and take note of our impact. As Bandura, the originator of the concept of collective efficacy, notes,

> Among the mechanisms of human agency, none is more central or pervasive than belief of personal efficacy. Unless people believe they can produce desired effects by their actions, they have little incentive to act, or to persevere in the face of difficulties. Whatever other factors serve as guides and motivators, they are rooted in the core belief

that one has the power to effect changes by
one's actions. (Bandura & Locke, 2003, p. 87)

Take a moment to consider the adults who make up the faculty and staff within your school community. Regardless of whether we are collaborating to serve our students from a physical school building or working together to meet our students' needs through distance education, if student engagement, learning, and growth is our ultimate goal, then together we must believe, our students must believe, and we must turn that belief into attitude with action.

And the "we" is crucial. Let us be clear: One person, believing on their own, can and will make a difference in the life of a child. A reminder of this is found in a saying commonly attributed to Dr. Seuss, suggesting, "To the world you may be one person, but to one person you may be the world." However, the power and purpose that come from all staff members collaborating, encouraging, and challenging each other, quintessentially being together in attitude and spirit, can make an impact on the entire school community, producing results beyond our wildest expectations. This is where turning attitude into action becomes a reality.

For example, we are certain that each of us has experienced a situation in our lives in which we were part of an effort to work together for the common good of others. Think back to a community service project in which you participated, a church activity, or a family outreach effort in which you took part. How did it feel to be working with others to make a positive difference? How do you suppose the person or group receiving the service felt? What positive outcomes may have resulted from your collective efforts? Please use the following space to write your reflections:

_____

_____

_____

_____

_____

_____

_____

_____

_____

_____

Now consider this question: Were there any individuals who were part of that group effort who are typically less engaged, less confident, or less assertive than they were during the joint effort to serve others? In many cases, we see people stand taller, speak louder, and smile more when they feel they are part of a productive team or working with others to achieve a positive outcome. This is true of our students as well. We turn our believing attitude into action by recognizing students' strengths and creating opportunities (learning opportunities can be as powerful as service opportunities) for those strengths to be leveraged. Consider the following response from Alex Gallegos, 17, in 2022 in an interview with Michelle:

> My teachers have ignited hope within me by affirming
> my ability to succeed after high school—which, in
> my case, includes achieving my dream of attending
> college, despite being a first-generation college
> student, a child of a split household, and a student
> receiving (proudly!) education in a majority

low-income community. Or perhaps because of those things, rather than despite them.

Alex says his teachers ignite hope by affirming his ability. They didn't question that he would be successful. They encouraged what he already knew about himself. Many of our students, however, need us to believe in them because often, they do not believe in themselves. In contrast to Alex, some of our students live with significant adversity and feel defeated or incapable. Michelle remembers a student sharing with her that he felt he had been "swimming against the current" since he was born. Another student told Michelle that she would never be able to succeed. She said, "You don't get it. I'm a failure. I've always failed. Nothin' I do will change that, so why should I even try?" Michelle also recalls a student who shouted, asking her to tell him he was "nothing." His reasoning was that it was "so obvious, I just want to hear you say it!" He was shocked when Michelle wouldn't comply, and he crumpled into tears at her encouragement that he was a valuable human being. We have all likely experienced a sense of helplessness or sadness as we interact with our students, listening and trying to learn from their heartaches and hardships. It is in this empathic response that we realize that our students may need us to recognize strengths for them to see them for themselves. For example, saying to a student, "You are so diligent in your work ethic! I hope you know that this trait will help you to be successful even when tasks are difficult," might buoy the student when frustrated or discouraged.

Intentionality ignites hope. Knowing our why, choosing to reframe the way we think and speak, and believing intentionally in ourselves and in our students are just a few ways that being intentional ignites hope in the midst of challenging situations. Likewise, elevating our adversity quotient requires that we cultivate courage.

IGNITE INTENTION

Please consider one way in which you will choose to ignite hope in the realm of *being intentional* for *one* student.

Student's first name or initial: _____

I will be more intentional with this student by (thinking, saying, being, or doing . . .):

_____

_____

_____

_____

_____

NOURISH!

At a time when educators often experience the feeling of being overwhelmed, we can further ignite hope in our own lives and the lives of others by nourishing our well-being. Reflecting upon Niebuhr's serenity prayer, we realize that when we are confronted with challenges in our lives, it is necessary to identify and accept with serenity the parts that we cannot change, the pieces that are out of our control. Serenity requires us to take a pause, to be still, to reflect, and to breathe. This is very challenging for some of us and requires intentional thought and action. Nancy makes this a daily habit to consider her day and note the wins. In fact, she makes a small note on her digital device before dinner each day about the wins—the things that went really, really well for the day. In doing so, she is continually reminded of the positive things in her life, and this fortifies her to accept and address the challenges she experiences.

We feel compelled to acknowledge that some of us and our students have experienced tragic events for which "accepting with serenity" does not come easily or immediately, if it comes at all. There are situations that people experience that are neglectful, abusive, traumatic, or even criminal. This type of harm can cause undue shame, a sense of helplessness, or genuine fear. In such situations, nurturing one's well-being may look like acknowledging that the situation truly is out of your control, it is not your fault, and that you cannot face it alone any longer. Cultivating courage in such a situation may mean choosing to trust someone from whom to seek support or help. This choice may feel impossible, yet it is within one's control and may be the first step toward finding serenity.

Regardless of how we pursue serenity, it takes vulnerability to identify situations that are predominantly out of our control and sincerely release them. We say this because it is difficult for some of us to admit that we do not have control over every piece of our lives—that, in fact, there are some situations, no matter what we say or do, that remain unchangeable. Researcher Brené Brown suggests, "Vulnerability is not weakness, it is our most accurate measure of courage" (Jensen, 2019). As such, when we lean into vulnerability, it compels us to ask ourselves if we are spending undue emotion and energy on that which is out of our control or negatively impacting our own well-being or the quality of our relationships. Likewise, it takes courageous vulnerability to ask ourselves if the way in which we responded to a situation, even one primarily out of our control, made matters worse. As we cultivate courage through vulnerability, we can focus with intention on the thoughts, words, behaviors, and situations over which we *do* have influence. For example, as school administrators, Nancy, Doug, and Michelle have all experienced moments in which they made decisions for staff or students in the moment, without taking time to consider the impact on all parties or seeking voice from those impacted by the decision. It is less complicated and expedient, at times, for an educational leader to make a decision on their own, yet that does not mean it is best for all involved. In fact, this type of decision can create frustration and divisiveness, limiting the potential investment of all and inhibiting a positive result. It is a vulnerable choice to admit when we are wrong in how we handled a situation, to seek sincere forgiveness, and request an opportunity to restart. At the same time, it is a courageous choice and one that will garner respect, restore harm, and open the door to a more effective and productive outcome.

The late great John Wooden advises, "Don't let what you cannot do interfere with what you can." Be intentional by asking yourself in a frustrating moment, What *can* I do? What is within my sphere of influence? Certainly, your attitude is something over which you have control. Could you practice gratitude more actively? Or might you take a few moments each morning to focus on reflections, affirmations, or prayer? Taking a moment to take an intentional breath when frustrated is also within your control. These intentional choices may seem insignificant, yet when put into practice with consistency, they will undoubtedly enhance your well-being and contribute to your ability to support the social and emotional needs of your students.

Consequently, we can make a choice to foster the well-being of our students simply by creating opportunities to learn two new things about each of them throughout the year. We can do this through individual conversations, or we can provide space for our students to write to us with prompts that include questions such as these:

▶ What is your favorite thing to do outside of school?

▶ What is a talent that you possess?

➤ What are two things that you would like me to know about you and how you learn best?

Likewise, making connections with families to let them know your desire to work with them in meeting the needs of their children is also a small act that can be initiated if you choose. The *way* in which you communicate is also in your purview and can impact the outcome and contribute to the well-being of others. Will you send an email, have a personal conversation, make a phone call, or write an old-fashioned letter? Will you measure your tone, own your part, and seek to understand? Ultimately, even when a situation is out of our control, there may be a fragment that we can influence to contribute to a more positive outcome.

Consider a situation in which you became focused on something that was *out* of your control that led to frustration, anger, or disappointment. Please explain the situation here:

_____

_____

_____

_____

_____

_____

_____

_____

_____

_____

Now take a moment to consider one concept—be it a thought, attitude, or action—that was *within* your control within that same situation. Is it possible that the situation might have changed for the better if you had focused on what was within your control? If so, what might it have looked like or how might it have impacted your feelings and why? Use this space to reflect.

_____

_____

_____

_____

_____

_____

_____

_____

_____

Consequently, we must be intentional in giving ourselves grace when experiencing feelings of overwhelmingness or inadequacy or in situations for which we made a regretful choice. For many of us, it is natural to offer grace or forgiveness to others, yet when it comes to offering it to ourselves, we can be resistant. We may not think we are worthy, or we may put unrealistic expectations on ourselves. We can nourish our well-being by leaning into the courage it may take to admit that we are human and that we get things wrong sometimes, to forgive ourselves so that we can move forward and contribute to a collaborative solution or foster an opportunity of growth for all involved. Most of us have experienced challenges that have left us feeling professionally overwhelmed, underprepared, and ineffective. As a result, we might have doubted our capabilities. If you have experienced such feelings or doubts, please know that this is natural, and you are not alone; but let us also remind you: You know your craft. As educators, we all do. We all have strengths. We are creative, intuitive, organized (some of us more than others!), and flexible. We have to be because we interact with children (and each other) every day.

Despite the uncertainty of a situation or type of adversity we encounter, we must remember that we have always known how to set and achieve goals. Our performance evaluations rely upon this fact. However, we now have a specific goal-setting process to practice and follow. When we feel overwhelmed or when we doubt ourselves, we can be intentional in setting a specific goal to practice self-compassion, for example, and reminding ourselves that one of our strengths as educators is to scaffold complexities in order for tangible objectives to be met. Our well-being and that of those with whom we interact will be nourished when we treat ourselves with the kindness, thoughtfulness, and the same grace we give to others.

NOURISH NOW

Please consider the content and reflections from the Nourish! section. Use the template on the following page to create a goal for yourself, specific to one new behavior in the realm of being intentional that will nourish your own well-being or that of your students.

Goal Statement:

SMART Goal Checklist: ☐ Specific ☐ Measurable ☐ Attainable
☐ Relevant ☐ Time-Bound

Why is this goal important?

How does this goal connect with my why?

What is my past experience or performance with this goal?

What are the benefits of my goal? What are the potential challenges or barriers?

How will I, or what skills/resources do I need, to measure, review, refine, and achieve my goal?

Action Steps:

1.

2.

3.

Start Date:

Review and Refine Date/s:

Completion Date:

ENGAGE!

Being intentional in the way we interact with our students can elevate their adversity quotient by impacting their sense of worth, providing opportunities to foster self-efficacy and agency, and engaging them in their own learning. Simply put, our intentional actions impact our students. For example, choosing to embrace clarity makes an impact on student engagement (Jensen, 2009). It is just one way to be intentional without complicating our workload or adding to the chaos or confusion that may already exist in our students' lives. An example of this is choosing to be clear and concise in the words we elect to use. Often, the number of words it takes for us to explain something is directly correlated to understanding. Fewer words result in less confusion. Be intentional in reminding yourself that, in many situations, less can be more. Shifting our mindset in the way we view a situation or being more intentional in our words and actions takes practice, and the effort is worth it, as it can be the difference between frustration or patience, judgment or acceptance, and hopelessness or hopefulness!

Moreover, as educators, we can be intentional in the way we design learning plans to provide opportunities for our students' strengths to shine. We realize this may take creativity, but as educators, this is one of *our* strengths. We can ask questions, facilitate discussions, and engage students in activities that highlight their strengths. We can reference specific examples that reinforce our belief in them. More specifically, leveraging students' strengths can foster student agency. Consequently, when we understand the importance of student agency, we can engage in intentional practices to foster our students' ability to manage and invest in their own learning.

EIGHT DIMENSIONS OF STUDENT AGENCY

Agency is central to a positive relationship to learning. Student agency is the management of own's own learning. Students with low levels of agency believe that learning is something that happens *to* them, and if they don't learn something, it is because of the teacher's inadequacies or their own traits. They don't see their own role in their learning.

Student agency is multidimensional and fostered by approaches to instruction, task design, motivation, assessment, and the development of study habits. These are also key for transfer of learning, which is the ability to apply knowledge and strategies under new conditions (National Research Council, 2012). Research on student agency in schools identified eight dimensions: self-efficacy, pursuit of interest, perseverance of effort, locus of control, mastery orientation, metacognition, self-regulation, and future orientation (Zeiser et al., 2018).

> **Self-efficacy.** The belief that one can achieve goals is fundamental to student agency, as it is with adults. The four sources of self-efficacy are having mastery experiences, seeing models, benefiting from social persuasion and encouragement, and knowing how to manage the physiological responses (Bandura, 1982). A student who possesses a higher level of self-efficacy believes that they can reach goals.

> **Pursuit of interest.** Think of this as a consistency of passion for a topic. We've seen the determination of students to learn everything there is to know about something that has seized their interest: coding, the *Titanic* disaster, geocaching, soccer. Students pursue their interests by reading books, talking with others about it, practice, and searching for new challenges that will build their skills. An important aspect of this is that they stick with some interests for a period of time and don't lose interest quickly (Peña & Duckworth, 2018).

Perseverance of effort. Hand-in-hand with interest is the willingness to continue on when something becomes more difficult. A student with a higher degree of persistence understands that setbacks can happen but is willing to see a project or task through to the end. Importantly, perseverance of effort can't be fostered when the tasks are not challenging. Unfortunately, this happens too often with some advanced students who skate through their years of schooling, only to discover that when they reach college they don't have the wherewithal or the resiliency to confront challenge.

Locus of control. The key word is "control"—to what extent does a learner believe that they are an influencer in the successful completion of the task? The location, or locus, of control speaks to where they attribute success and failure. A person with a strong internal locus of control places a higher value on their own skills and effort, while those with an external locus of control focus on the difficulty of the project or what other people's skill levels are. In truth, locus of control is on a continuum rather than an internal/external binary. An internal locus of control is associated with higher levels of achievement (Shepherd et al., 2006).

Mastery orientation. Goals drive all of us, but there is also the motivation for those goals. The beliefs we have about our goals orient us onto a path. The goals of students can fall broadly into two paths: a mastery orientation or a performance orientation (Pintrich, 2003). Students with a mastery orientation understand that what they are learning benefits them. They understand that learning a topic in one class will benefit them in another. As well, they judge their own performance in terms of what they have learned, not in comparison to others. A student with a mastery orientation says, "I want to learn Spanish so I can speak to my grandparents." Students with a performance orientation have goals, too, but they may be tied more closely to the amount of effort required and their standing with others. A student with a performance orientation may say, "I want to pass Spanish class," or "I want to get an A in this class so I can move up in the class ranking."

Metacognition. Often described as "thinking about thinking," metacognition develops in the first years of schooling and continues across a lifetime. You'll notice this happening with the five-year-old that checks the picture on a puzzle box lid to complete it. Metacognitive strategies are embedded in instruction. We teach early readers to monitor their understanding so that when they lose meaning in a text they go back to re-read. We teach older students to take notes and use them as part of their studying. A student with a higher degree of metacognition will notice what is confusing, ask questions, and mentally summarize what they are learning.

Self-regulation. Closely related to metacognition is the self-regulation needed to learn. A student with a higher degree of self-regulation can reset their attention during math when they notice they're thinking instead about a video game. Self-regulation plays an important role in practice and studying. For instance, being organized, keeping track of assignments, and setting aside time for study are all essential skills.

Future orientation. Perceptions of what constitutes the future are definitely going to vary with age. Young children may consider the future to be lunchtime. But a goal of schooling is to help students see that the learning they do today is grounded not only in their current context but also in their investment in their own future aspirations. Early-grades social studies curriculum includes study of different occupations and community roles, and lots of schools host Career Days so that children can ask questions about how the firefighter decided on that professional field. Middle and high school efforts include helping students develop résumés and introducing academic and extracurricular efforts that will burnish their postsecondary applications. Students with a future orientation are able to equate their school efforts and experiences as a foundation for adult aspirations.

TEACHER PRACTICES TO BUILD STUDENT AGENCY

Teachers play an important role in the relative amount of agency a student possesses. The amount of autonomy experienced by students has a direct link to their sense of agency (Filippello et al., 2019). Teaching styles that are highly controlling place a premium on compliance, convey approval that is dependent on achievement, and ignore students who do not achieve, resulting in a "chilly" classroom climate. These teaching behaviors foster an external locus of control that is authority-based, and students in these classrooms grow more insecure about their learning and their ability to take action. The result can often be learned helplessness.

In contrast, teaching styles that increase students' autonomy foster those who have a higher sense of agency (Filippello et al., 2019). These autonomy-supportive classrooms are led by teachers who encourage discussion, listen for students' points of view, make feedback informative, and take the time to link student actions to their success. Choice and relevance are crucial curricular features. Importantly, in doing so they help students develop an internal locus of control. For a student who has had a compromised relationship to learning, autonomy-supportive classrooms can be transformative.

The intentional use of teacher practices specifically aimed at building student agency have shown promising results over time, as short as within a single school year (Zeiser et al., 2018). Given that the building of student agency can fuel student learning, this is an investment that can deliver measurable results. In this lesson and those that follow, we will discuss application through a menu of actions and practices that educators can use. The following menu is specific to the intentional teacher practice of building student agency and is clustered into three categories: student opportunities, student-teacher collaboration, and teacher-led approaches. To what degree are these practices part of your daily instruction?

Menu of Practices That Build Student Agency			
Use the checklist to reflect on your current practices as they relate to teaching about and creating opportunities for agency.			
Use the following reflection scale:			
1: *I consistently create opportunities for this to occur in my instructional setting.*			
2: *I sometimes create opportunities for this to occur in my instructional setting.*			
3: *I rarely or never create opportunities for this to occur in my instructional setting.*			
Student Opportunities	1	2	3
Choice. Students make choices about content and process of their work.	☐	☐	☐
Group work. Students have opportunities to work in groups to learn and practice agency necessary for group success.	☐	☐	☐
Harnessing outside opportunities. Students have opportunities to demonstrate agency outside the classroom and make connections to its application in the classroom.	☐	☐	☐
Revision. Students are able to revise assignments or tests after they receive feedback.	☐	☐	☐
Student self-reflection. Students self-reflect using journals, logs, or other structured templates or tools.	☐	☐	☐

Student Opportunities	1	2	3
Student-led instruction. Students demonstrate agency by leading instruction on a particular skill or concept.	☐	☐	☐
Student-Teacher Collaboration			
Developing relationships. Teachers develop personal relationships with students to better understand their agency strengths, needs, and motivators.	☐	☐	☐
Feedback. Teachers provide students with feedback and scaffold the process of students seeking feedback.	☐	☐	☐
Goal-setting. Teachers help students set goals to complete coursework while improving agency.	☐	☐	☐
Individual conferences. Teachers hold one-on-one meetings with students to discuss elements of student agency and its relationship to academic work.	☐	☐	☐
Student voice. Teachers provide students with opportunities to contribute to and provide feedback on key decisions in the classroom.	☐	☐	☐
Teacher-Led Approaches			
Assessment. Teachers design to evaluate student agency.	☐	☐	☐
Direct instruction. Teachers provide explicit instruction to develop skills related to student agency.	☐	☐	☐
Modeling. Teachers model agency to demonstrate it to students in a meaningful context.	☐	☐	☐
Positive reinforcement. Teachers provide positive reinforcement for demonstration of agency.	☐	☐	☐

(Continued)

(Continued)

Teacher-Led Approaches	1	2	3
Scaffolding. Teachers provide students with tools, strategies, and resources to help scaffold students toward mastery of agency.	☐	☐	☐
Verbal cues. Teachers provide brief spoken prompts in real time to highlight or remind students of behaviors that demonstrate agency.	☐	☐	☐

Adapted from: Zeiser, K., Scholz, C., & Cirks, V. (2018). *Maximizing student agency: Implementing and measuring student-centered learning practices.* American Institutes of Research (p. 30). https://files.eric.ed.gov/fulltext/ED592084.pdf.

ENGAGE EXTENSION

Please consider your responses to the Menu of Practices That Build Student Agency and respond to the following prompts:

My current practices reflect strengths in the following areas:

_____

_____

_____

_____

_____

I notice that I rarely, if ever, create opportunities for (choose one for which you checked "3"):

_____

_____

_____

_____

_____

I will begin providing opportunities to practice what I noticed above by (specifically doing what?):

_____

_____

_____

_____

_____

Thank you. Before we move on, take a moment to take an intentional breath. Do this by setting this book aside, closing your eyes, breathing in through your nose, holding it for two to three seconds, and breathing out through your mouth. Ready, go . . .

Welcome back! Taking an intentional breath at any time, but especially when we feel overwhelmed, frustrated, or confused, helps us to center, relax, and focus, not only positively impacting our state of mind and body but also that of those with whom we are interacting.

LESSON REFLECTION

This lesson introduced various strategies for igniting hope, nourishing well-being, and engaging students in the face of adversity. To culminate the lesson, please consider the following table indicating specific actions that foster intentionality in the face of adversity, preparing us to be at our best as human beings and instructional leaders. At the same time, consider the divergent actions that can derail our journey to persevere when we experience hardships, challenges, or trauma, compromising our ability to teach, lead, and support others. Then, use the blank spaces to identify acts or behaviors specific to your way of being that foster intentionality, as well as those that interfere in your capacity to act with intention.

Actions That Foster Intentionality	Actions That Derail Intentionality

In your final reflection of this lesson, consider one intentional mindset and/or behavior you would like to *stop, start,* and *continue.* Choose one to *stop* because, upon reflection, you realize it may lead to frustration, judgment, or hopelessness. Choose one mindset or behavior you would like to *start* practicing in an effort to be more mindful or intentional, and one mindset or behavior you realize you do well and want to *continue.* For example: I tend to focus on Jerrod's negative behaviors. I'm going to **stop** calling him out for being disruptive in front of his peers. I'm going to **start** looking for a positive character trait to attribute to Jerrod and verbally acknowledge that trait during class to reinforce positive behavior. I will **continue** to care about Jerrod's performance in my class. Or: I will **stop** looking at my phone while walking in the hallway. I will **start** acknowledging people by name while passing. I will **continue** to use my students' names when I greet them each day.

Please personalize your answers below:

STOP:

_____

_____

_____

_____

_____

START:

_____

_____

_____

_____

_____

CONTINUE:

_____

_____

_____

_____

_____

In the long run, choosing to be intentional in focusing on that which is within our control promotes our well-being and helps us to believe in ourselves and our ability to make an impact on our students' lives and learning. We encourage you to share these ideas with your colleagues so they, too, will feel empowered. Ultimately, when we all step forward together, choosing to be intentional in our thoughts, words, and actions, believing in our students and ourselves, we will galvanize ourselves and each other, and we *will* ignite hope, nourish well-being, and elevate the adversity quotient!

CORE CONNECTION

Control is our ability to take command of situations and our responses to those situations. We recognize what we can control in a situation rather than becoming overwhelmed by things that are beyond our control (Stoltz, 1997).

Being intentional in our thoughts, words, and behaviors can elevate our ability to respond to adverse situations in a way that helps rather than hinders. Practicing collective efficacy while modeling and teaching self-efficacy and agency leverages the control dimension of the adversity quotient. Likewise, cultivating courage by pursuing serenity, identifying opportunities for change, and then taking action through intentionality fosters our ability to confront adversity with calm, perseverance, and fortitude. Finally, being intentional about *why* we do what we do allows us to connect with the purpose and meaning of our vocations, nurturing our well-being and our vocational resilience and helping us to be more joyful, motivated, effective, and productive.

2

CREATE CONNECTIONS

I've learned that people will forget what you said, people will forget what you did, but people will never forget how you made them feel.

—Maya Angelou

According to the National Scientific Council on the Developing Child (2015),

> Despite the widespread belief that individual grit, extraordinary self-reliance, or some in-born, heroic strength of character can triumph over calamity, science now tells us that it is the reliable presence of at least one supportive relationship and multiple opportunities for developing effective coping skills that are essential building blocks for the capacity to do well in the face of significant adversity. (p. 7)

This science tells us relationships matter! Pursuing intentional change by actively creating connections with others is a way in which we can ignite hope—not only in the lives of our students, but in our own lives as well!

PROMPTS TO PONDER

- What does creating connections mean to you?
- How might creating more intentional connections with your colleagues impact your ability to respond to challenging life or work situations?
- Is there anything you would like to cultivate the courage to change in the way in which you connect with others?
- How might creating connections with your students elevate their ability to respond with determination and perseverance in the face of adversity?

IGNITE!

As educators, we are well aware of the value of positive relationships. Nevertheless, we often become so enmeshed in all that we must *do* that we forget or neglect to simply *be*. Take a moment to consider the very act of being and ask yourself, What is my typical way of *being* in how I speak, act, and interact with others? Our *way of being* can impact the outcome of our experiences and the authenticity of our relationships. And the best part is that our state of being already exists. It is not something more we have to do, rather it is inherent to our ever-waking moment. The key, however, is to increase our awareness of *how* we experience being.

Being authentically connected requires that we are present, and for some of us, being present necessitates that we are still. We realize that being still can be a challenge within itself. Yet we contend that when we choose to be present, we can create intentional connections with others that have the power to result in healthy, reliable relationships. This outcome is paramount to elevating one's ability to respond to significant life challenges because when trustworthy relationships exist, people within those relationships realize they are not alone.

This realization can bring hope to what may have felt like a hopeless situation. It can provide reassurance that one will be supported through pain and encouraged through hardships.

At the same time, we can be the spark of hope in someone's life, even if a trustworthy relationship has not yet been achieved, by being intentional about the little things. There are opportunities for sincere connectedness every day that we often miss in our busyness. For example, how many of us pass a colleague or student in the hall at school and as we are walking by one another say, "Hi! How are you?" A missed opportunity occurs when we keep walking! The question "How are you?" has become a greeting in our society today. We must remember that it is a question. If we are going to ask the question, it is essential that we stop and listen to the answer with as much physical, mental, and emotional presence we have available to infuse into that moment.

When we do this, we invite an earnest connection that can impact a person's feelings and experience of the world around them. This deliberate interaction lets them know that someone truly does care about how they are doing. As such, they may be more inclined to share beyond, "I'm fine," which is the typical response, whether true or not, when the question is asked while passing by.

If, on the other hand, we do not have the capacity to be present, then instead of asking, "How are you?" we encourage you to express a wish for a nice day or share a positive comment. If you know the person, use their name when you offer this greeting. The use of a person's name communicates "I see you and you matter." In psychology, this is known as immediacy, or our accessibility and relatability. People judge our immediacy when we do things such as this:

➤ Gesture when talking
➤ Look at people and smile while talking
➤ Use names

- Use "we" and "us" to refer to the group

- Invite people to provide feedback

- Use vocal variety (pauses, inflections, stress, emphasis) when talking to the group

Consider this list. Is there one behavior that you engage in consistently? If so, please share on the following lines what it looks like in your realm of influence. Is there one behavior upon which you could be more intentional? What might it look like during a typical school day if you were to begin engaging in this behavior? Please reflect here:

_____

_____

_____

_____

_____

_____

_____

_____

Furthermore, we can ignite hope in the lives of our students and our families when we are socially aware. Socially aware connections mean being open-minded and open-hearted to cultures, religions, sexual orientations, gender identities, traditions and lifestyles, and socio-economic statuses unlike our own, as well as to others' points of view and life experiences. It might look like this: "I don't really understand where you're coming from, but I want to. Can you tell me more?" *Tell me more*, we believe, is a powerful phrase because it allows us to be vulnerable.

Vulnerability is a choice that accepts that these three words take away our need to prove our point or even our need to be *right*. *Tell me more* isn't accusatory; it does not create defensiveness because *tell me more* lives on common ground, the same place empathy lives. *Tell me more* says, "We are both human beings, and I care about you, even if I don't know what you are going through. I am here. I am with you, I accept you for who you are, and I want to understand." By truly listening, by seeking to understand—leaning into conflict, discomfort, inexperience, or lack of awareness—we can ignite hope. At the same time, leaning into such situations calls for us to cultivate courage to, as Reinhold Niebuhr suggests, "change the things I can." Being an active participant in contributing to an educational system that is equitable for all students is one of those things. During a personal interview in 2022, Dr. Kori Hamilton Biagas, founder of Just Educators, reminded us,

> *We are all a part of the system that perpetuates oppression of "othered" children, and we participate in that system admittedly or not. If we truly care for and love our students, we will set aside our own discomfort to disrupt and dismantle a system that consistently does not serve them.*

We wonder if we can apply Biagas's challenge regarding children to all people. What if we strive to create connections with other humans even when we are uncomfortable, even when we don't know what to say or how to act? What if we demonstrate courageous vulnerability by admitting that we are unsure of the best way to address a conversation or situation? What if we ask for help? Action in response to all these questions will help us to open our entire beings—our eyes, minds, and hearts—as we pursue genuine human connection.

Additionally, we won't know what our students or colleagues are experiencing, what adversity they may be facing, until we choose to build relationships with them. We will never know what a student, family, or colleague may or may not need—emotionally, physically, or financially—if we don't first connect with them on a human level, expressing genuine interest and compassion. There may be educators among us who claim "it is not my job" to consider the needs of students beyond academics. We have learned throughout our years in education that those who cannot see the importance of building relationships, supporting others through personal challenges, and being *there* to encourage and empower will have difficulty engaging students academically, gaining support from students' families, and working collaboratively with colleagues.

In a personal interview between Michelle and Maurice Elias, Dr. Elias captured the importance of being intentional in our efforts to create connection when he suggested, "Listen carefully to what others are saying—look for the value in their words, even if you usually do not find their positions agree with yours. What can you connect to in what you are hearing? Genuine connection is the foundation on which hope is built."

IGNITE INTENTION

Please consider one way in which you will choose to ignite hope by creating a more intentional connection with just one student.

Student's first name or initial: _____

I will create an intentional connection with this student by (thinking, saying, being, or doing . . .):

_____

_____

_____

_____

_____

NOURISH!

Choosing to make intentional connections inevitably nurtures our well-being and that of those with whom we interact. Neuroscience tells us that when we make a positive social connection with another human being, we experience a release of neurotransmitters in our brain such as dopamine, serotonin, and oxytocin that help us to feel positive, more focused, and better able to concentrate, while cortisol, our primary stress hormone, is reduced. Smiling is a fundamental example of positive social connection that can nourish our own well-being and that of those with whom we interact. Think about a time when someone sincerely smiled at you, and we are emphasizing *sincerely* here. Picture a smile that starts in someone's heart and expresses joy not only through their smile but also through their eyes. In this situation, you can't help but smile too—even if you didn't originally feel like smiling! Another person's sincere action can have a significant affect on our emotions and our response.

Likewise, one's well-being can be nurtured by making the conscious choice to be *with* others when we are struggling, rather than going it alone. With this in mind, it is essential that we establish the difference between being alone and feeling alone. Although making space and setting boundaries to carve out "alone" time is essential to protecting our well-being, if one feels lonely, it is different. Feeling alone, especially when experiencing substantial adversity, can lead to sadness, loneliness, and depression. It can cause us to isolate and ultimately compromise our mental health, as well as our emotional, spiritual, social, and physical states of being. Surrounding ourselves with friends or loved ones can create a sense of confidence that is found in togetherness—a knowledge that others are available to encourage us, stand by us, or help to carry our pain. On the other hand, if friends or family are not present or available, we must garner our courage—and our humility—to ask another for help, perhaps from a colleague, supervisor, or mental health professional. We realize most educators have servants' hearts and are very willing to be there for others. Yet many of us are reticent to ask for support or even admit that we need it. Reaching out to another, acknowledging the need for care, comfort, or guidance does not make us weak. It only makes us human.

This undeniable fact of our humanity reminds us that physical connection is paramount to the nourishment of one's well-being as well. Innately, physical touch offers tangible evidence that we are not alone in the world. On a scientific level, research indicates that physical touch stimulates the release of oxytocin, which is a chemical that is produced in the hypothalamus and released into the bloodstream as a neurotransmitter by the pituitary gland. As a neurotransmitter, oxytocin can promote a sense of well-being, relaxation, trust, and overall psychological stability, as it decreases stress and anxiety (Watson, 2023). That said, the simple act of a sincere handshake can boost our well-being and that of the person with whom we are physically connecting. Consider this: When we reach out to another human being to shake hands, our hand must be open. Sadly, so often in the world today, we live our lives with metaphorical closed fists. When we rush through life, checking off our lists, walking right by those in need without even a glance, our hands and hearts are closed. When we feel frustrated by or even angry at a family member or neighbor because their political views do not align with our own, our minds are closed and our fists are clenched. When we fail to see through the eyes of another because their ethnicity, race, religion, sexual orientation, gender identity, or experiences are different than ours or when we choose to ignore oppression or allow our discomfort to paralyze our integrity, our entire beings are closed. The act of a handshake not only initiates the release of oxytocin and the benefits that follow, but it can also catalyze social-emotional connection in the mere gesture of reaching out with an open hand.

Let's take a moment to reflect. Are there any specific ways you can identify in which you lived your life with your hands, eyes, heart, and mind open? Can you think of an example from your life of a situation that began with a handshake, but ultimately led to an act of connection in which you demonstrated empathy, established mutual respect, leaned into discomfort, or learned more about something or someone? Please share your reflections here:

_____

_____

_____

_____

_____

_____

_____

_____

_____

Consequently, this openness and reliability that can be elicited from a handshake can also promote trust. Trustworthiness is paramount to sustainable relationships because it is a primary foundation upon which relationships are built. We have all seen marriages falter or dissolve when trust is broken. Tension between teens and their parents often lies on the path of trust or lack thereof. Even corporations rely on trustworthy relationships to attain profit. In fact, the most successful businesses will attest to the fact that branding, or even the product itself, is insignificant compared to the relationships that the business owner and employees build with each other and their customers. The same is true within school communities. When trust is present, staff, students, and even their families are more inclined to fully invest and actively participate in the vision and goals of the school, contributing to a school culture that is supportive of everyone's well-being. Experts from American Institutes for Research studied relationships as drivers of human development—specifically how relationships and context shape learning and development (Osher et al., 2018). They found relationships that are based on trust, as well as those that are reciprocal, attuned, and culturally responsive, are a positive driver of learning and development. Furthermore, "Such relationships help to establish idiographic developmental pathways that serve as the foundation for life-long learning, adaptation, the integration of social, affective, emotional, and cognitive processes" (Osher et al., 2018, p. 8).

More specifically, Nese et al. (2022) conducted a study implementing the inclusive skill-building learning approach (ISLA), in which preventative strategies and instructional responses for teachers and school staff were carried out with intention based on three specific strategies. The three strategies are represented by the acronym WOW, which stands for

- Welcome students at the door,
- Own your environment and establish and teach routines, and
- Wrap up class with intention.

According to the study, "the implementation of WOW strategies supports the development of clear classroom procedures and embedding intentional opportunities to nourish support with daily caring interactions with adults." When implemented with fidelity, these strategies resulted in improved prosocial skills, behavior, and attendance; more instructional minutes; and less exclusionary practices such as suspension or expulsion.

Furthermore, students participating in this study expressed a more optimistic outlook on future academic outcomes, as well as greater receptiveness to attending and participating in class when teachers "engaged with them in a caring, kind, humorous, and/or calm way" (Nese et al., 2021). Simply stated, when teachers and school staff are consistent in their effort to connect with authenticity and intention, it can foster well-being for all.

That said, educators commonly acknowledge that, when stressed, overwhelmed, or experiencing significant adversity themselves, it is more challenging to act in a way that demonstrates genuine kindness, compassion, serenity, or humor, let alone consistently maintain procedures such as the WOW approach. Yet it is, in fact, approaches such as WOW and the genuine physiological, social, and emotional interactions that result from such practices that nurture educator well-being and prepare administrators, teachers, and school staff to better support the academic, social, and emotional well-being of their students.

NOURISH NOW

Consider the various content, behaviors, and/or strategies discussed in this section. Please take a moment to use the following template to create a goal for yourself specific to one new behavior for creating intentional connections that will nourish your own well-being or that of your students.

Goal Statement:

SMART Goal Checklist: ☐ Specific ☐ Measurable ☐ Attainable
☐ Relevant ☐ Time-Bound

Why is this goal important?

How does this goal connect with my why?

What is my past experience or performance with this goal?

What are the benefits of my goal? What are the potential challenges or barriers?

How will l, or what skills/resources do I need, to measure, review, refine, and achieve my goal?

Action Steps:
1.
2.
3.

Start Date:

Review and Refine Date/s:

Completion Date:

ENGAGE!

Creating positive connections is of utmost importance in developing nurturing, mutually respectful relationships with our students. In fact, student achievement, growth, and engagement can be a direct reflection of students' connections to teachers. Educators can create connections in a myriad of ways. Consider this response obtained from an interview with teacher David Trujillo:

> I create connections by trying to find something in common with my students. If we don't seem to have anything in common, I ask them about their interests and have them share their passions so I can learn from them. I make a concerted effort to show my passion for learning and exude this through my teaching. I am enthusiastic and try to excite students with my passion and animation about my content matter. I make things real by having students connect with something personal within each lesson. Furthermore, I give them positive reinforcement so they can develop a passion for learning. I also laugh with my students. I tease with them and let them tease with me. It seems like a small thing, but it makes a difference with behavior and academic performance.

Mr. Trujillo reminds us that seeking commonalities, showing interest, sharing passion, and having fun with students are all ways to create connections. Likewise, taking time each day to greet our students and our colleagues by name helps them to feel acknowledged and recognized. It doesn't matter if it occurs in person or virtually; it only matters *that* it occurs! Communicating in this way creates connection, as does communication through active listening, mailing student appreciation or recognition postcards home, making positive phone calls, or sharing celebratory announcements to recognize positive behavior, personal talents, or academic accomplishments. The powerful result of authentic connection positively impacts the person with whom we are connecting but also alters our state of mind and being for the better.

Take a moment to reflect on someone from your experience as a learner who had a positive impact on your life. How did that person connect with you? What traits did that person possess? Have you applied anything from this experience to your own role as a teacher, staff member, counselor, or leader now? Please share your thoughts here:

_____

_____

_____

_____

_____

_____

_____

_____

_____

FIVE ELEMENTS OF TEACHER-STUDENT RELATIONSHIPS

People learn better when they have a positive relationship with the person providing instruction. Here are five important elements of teacher-student relationships (Cornelius-White, 2007, p. 113):

1. *Teacher empathy*—understanding

2. *Unconditional positive regard*—warmth

3. *Genuineness*—the teacher's self-awareness

4. *Non-directivity*—student-initiated and student-regulated activities

5. *Encouragement of critical thinking*—as opposed to traditional memory emphasis

These student-centered practices are essential in any classroom. Establishing these conditions begins from the first interactions students have with the teacher:

➤ Strong teacher-student relationships rely on effective communication and a willingness to address issues that strain the relationship.

➤ Positive relationships are fostered and maintained when teachers set fair expectations, involve students in determining aspects of the classroom organization and management, and hold students accountable for the expectations in an equitable way.

➤ Importantly, relationships are not destroyed when problematic behaviors occur, either on the part of the teacher or students. This is an important point for educators. If we want to ensure students read, write, communicate, and think at high levels, we have to develop positive, trusting relationships with *each* student.

Just as important, high levels of positive relationships build trust and make your classroom a safe place to explore what the students do not know, their errors and misconceptions. Indeed, powerful student-teacher relationships allow errors to be seen as opportunities to learn. A lot of students (and teachers) avoid situations where they are likely to make errors or feel challenged with exposing their lack of knowledge or understanding, but we want to turn these situations into powerful learning opportunities, and this is more likely to occur in high-trust environments. And it is not just high positive levels of teacher–student relations, but how you develop high-trust environments so one student can talk about their struggles of learning with other students and the notion of "struggle" becomes a positive and fun activity (Hamre & Pianta, 2010).

For students experiencing significant adversity, relationships matter. When students experience positive relationships with teachers, not only is their ability to learn enhanced, but their ability to regulate their behavior can also improve, contributing to a more productive and positive classroom climate. Such climates can create improved cognitive and academic competence, self-efficacy, behavior, engagement, and attendance (Norton Hamre et al., 2013). Thus, teachers who engage in practices that create connection and build relationships with every student cultivate opportunities to optimize the learning environment for all. Use the following Menu of Practices to reflect on your current practices as they relate to creating opportunities for connection by establishing (or reestablishing) relationships with students. Add ideas if you have them as you engage in the self-assessment.

Menu of Practices That Build Healthy, Growth-Producing Relationships

Use the following reflection scale:

1: *I consistently create opportunities for this to occur in my instructional setting.*

2: *I sometimes create opportunities for this to occur in my instructional setting.*

3: *I rarely or never create opportunities for this to occur in my instructional setting.*

Teacher Empathy: *Teachers provide opportunities for students to seek connection.*	1	2	3
Greet each student at the door (at the beginning of each day or period) by using students' names.	☐	☐	☐
Establish and review classroom expectations or agreements.	☐	☐	☐
Begin lessons with a positive affirmation (e.g., favorite quotes, a silly joke, short video messages).	☐	☐	☐
Create opportunities for students to check-in (e.g., one word that represents . . . or "would you rather" question).	☐	☐	☐
Create an opportunity each morning for students to *confidentially* rate their readiness to learn (e.g., use of numerical or emotion-rating scale).	☐	☐	☐
Establish a specific time each week to check-in with families to share a positive message about their student.	☐	☐	☐
Ask students to complete an interest survey or to share a written reflection of their interests, hobbies, strengths, and needs.	☐	☐	☐
Additional ideas:			
Unconditional Positive Regard: *How will your students know you care about them as people?*			
Weave into lessons what you have learned about students' pursuit through interest surveys or individual written reflections.	☐	☐	☐
Create opportunities to provide one-on-one verbal feedback on individual student work so that they can hear the expression in your voice, rather than read your written feedback without context.	☐	☐	☐

(Continued)

(Continued)

Unconditional Positive Regard: *How will your students know you care about them as people?*	1	2	3
Create a space in the classroom for students to post accomplishments. Encourage students to add written work, artwork, or earned certificates or awards.	☐	☐	☐
Additional ideas:	☐	☐	☐

Genuineness: *How will your students know you care about yourself as a professional?*			
Dress and groom professionally.	☐	☐	☐
Project a demeanor that is optimistic about them and you.	☐	☐	☐
Share your passion for your subject, your students, or education in general.	☐	☐	☐
Make it clear in words and actions that your instructional space is a place for students to learn about themselves, the world, and each other.	☐	☐	☐
Practice courageous vulnerability to let students know when you are experiencing stress or need to take a breath to reset. (Remember, students don't need details, but they do respect general transparency.)	☐	☐	☐
Model traits that nourish well-being, such as being reflective, intentional, and accountable.	☐	☐	☐
Additional ideas:	☐	☐	☐

Non-Directivity: How will your students know you hold their abilities in high regard?	1	2	3
Hold individual conversations with students to help them identify their strengths, goals, and growth areas.	☐	☐	☐
Ask questions that mediate the student's thinking, rather than asking leading questions.	☐	☐	☐
Use shared decision-making about curriculum or class responsibilities with students.	☐	☐	☐
Additional ideas:	☐	☐	☐

Encouragement of Critical Thinking: How will your students know that you value their learning process?			
Foster discussion among peers using questions that expand their thinking (e.g., open-ended questions that have many correct responses or many ways to solve).	☐	☐	☐
Every lesson includes opportunities for students to write about, illustrate, or discuss their thinking with peers.	☐	☐	☐
Build choice and relevance into assignments and projects.	☐	☐	☐
Additional ideas:	☐	☐	☐

PEER-TO-PEER RELATIONSHIPS

Teacher-student relationships influence peer perceptions of classmates. When a student asks a question indicating they are lost, do not know where they are going, or are just plain wrong, high levels of peer-to-peer relationships mean that this student is not ridiculed, does not feel that they should be silent and bear their not-knowing alone, and can depend on the teacher and often other students to help them out.

Unfortunately, in some cases, specific students are targeted for behavioral correction while other students engaged in the same behavior are not noticed. We recall a primary grade classroom in which a student was repeatedly chastised for a problematic behavior, but when other children engaged in the same, their behavior was ignored and allowed to continue. And the children noticed. As one of the students said, "Mr. Henderson doesn't want Cameron in our class." It's hard to develop positive relationships, and then achieve, when you are not wanted.

A teacher's dislike for a student is rarely a secret to classmates. Students are exquisitely attuned to the emotions of the teacher. Think about it: They are observing us closely day after day, and they get very good at being able to read the social environment. They watch how we interact verbally and nonverbally with classmates. We are actually modeling how peers should interact with the specific student. Sadly, students who are disliked by the teacher are more readily rejected by peers than those who are liked by the teacher (Birch & Ladd, 1997). This phenomenon, called *social referencing*, is especially influential among children, who turn to adults to decide what they like and do not like. Elementary students can accurately state who is disliked by their teacher. In a study of 1,400 fifth graders, the students reported that they also did not like the children that the teachers told the researchers that they did not like. As the researchers noted, the "targeted" students were held in negative regard six months later, even though they were now in a new grade level with a different teacher (Hendrikx et al., 2017). Much like a pebble dropped into a pond, being disliked by the teacher ripples across other social relationships and endures well beyond the time span of a negative interaction.

A study of differential teacher treatment of students found that low-achieving students (Good, 1987)

- Are criticized more often for failure.
- Are praised less frequently.
- Receive less feedback.
- Are called on less often.
- Have less eye contact from the teacher.
- Have fewer friendly interactions with the teacher.
- Experience acceptance of their ideas less often.

There is another term for this: a "chilly" classroom climate in which some students do not feel they are valued and instead feel that "their presence . . . is at best peripheral, and at worst an unwelcome intrusion" (Hall & Sandler, 1982, p. 3). We do not in any way believe that these differential teacher behaviors are conscious and intentional. One speculation is that because educators don't feel successful with students they view as lower achieving, we subconsciously avoid contact with them. After all, we were human beings long before we became educators, and as social animals, we attempt to surround ourselves with people who make us feel good about ourselves. Students who are not making gains make us feel like failures, and so we detach ourselves even more.

Now view Good's list from the opposite direction—students we see as being high achieving get more of us. Our attention, our contact, our interactions are more frequent, sustained, and growth-producing. It is understandable that we gravitate to those students that make us feel successful as educators. But it is also a version of the Matthew effect, this time in attention rather than reading—the rich get richer while the poor get poorer (Stanovich, 1986). In this case, it's our positive attention that is gold.

ENGAGE EXTENSION

Please consider your responses to the Menu of Practices That Build Healthy, Growth-Producing Relationships, as well as the content related to peer-to-peer relations and respond to the following prompts.

My current practices reflect strengths in the following areas:

_____

_____

_____

_____

_____

I notice that I rarely, if ever, create opportunities for (choose one for which you checked "3" or one suggestion from peer-to-peer relations content):

_____

_____

_____

_____

I will begin providing opportunities to practice what I noticed above by (specifically doing what?):

_____

_____

_____

_____

_____

LESSON REFLECTION

In reflection of this lesson, please take a moment to note specific actions in the following table that foster connection and, in doing so, nourish our well-being or that of others during adverse experiences. At the same time, contemplate specific actions that could derail opportunities to connect with others in situations that cause us to feel overwhelmed, frustrated, helpless, or hopeless. Identify any actions that resonate with you or cause you to be curious. Then, fill in the blank spaces with acts or behaviors specific to your way of being that cultivate your relationships and foster productive classroom culture or teamwork, as well as some in the opposing column that contribute to derailing your ability to face your own adversity with the support of others or those acts that may prevent you from providing support to your students in times of need.

Actions That Foster Connections	Actions That Derail Connections

As you did in Lesson One, please consider one intentional mindset and/or behavior you would like to *stop, start,* and *continue* in the sphere of creating and building connections and relationships. Choose one to *stop* because, upon reflection, you realize your thoughts, words, or behavior limit positive relational or academic impact. Choose one mindset or behavior you would like to *start* promoting intentional relational connections, and one mindset or behavior you realize you practice well and want to *continue.*

Please personalize your answers here:

STOP:

_____

_____

_____

_____

_____

START:

_____

_____

_____

_____

_____

CONTINUE:

_____

_____

_____

_____

_____

Creating connections can empower us to pursue intentional change in the way in which we respond to substantial challenges and adversities. We have all experienced the reality of the common mantra, *Better together.* We all possess individual strengths and areas of our lives in which we can grow. Connecting with others allows us to share our strengths and to lend a hand or cultivate courage to seek support. Who we are and how we interact with the human beings within our school community can foster well-being and empower ourselves and our students to engage socially, emotionally, and academically, leading to an encounter with learning and living in which all are invested, creating a life-changing impact that reaches beyond the school experience.

CORE CONNECTION

Reach is our ability to respond to adverse situations and seek help and support when needed. We build a network of supportive relationships and resources to reduce the feelings of isolation, or we find support and guidance to help us overcome challenges (Stoltz, 1997).

Being connected neutralizes isolation, which is vital because the lack of human connection can lead to loneliness, anxiety, depression, and additional experiences that negatively impact our overall well-being. Being connected, therefore, can grow relationships, increase feelings of belonging, improve our own self-worth and self-efficacy, and extend our **reach**. Cultivating the courage to make intentional connections can grow empathy, trust, and agency, thus improving student/educator or collegial relationships. Finally, creating connections can elevate our adversity quotient (AQ) by expanding our reach in the way in which we respond to substantial adverse experiences. Developing our reach increases our ability to recognize that we are not alone while facing hardships, to allow ourselves to be vulnerable as we seek support or guidance from another, and to sustain trustworthy relationships, ultimately building a foundation upon which to raise our AQ.

3

SEEK TO UNDERSTAND

It is not our differences that divide us. It is our inability to recognize, accept, and celebrate those differences.

—Audre Lorde

Seek first to understand, then to be understood.

—Stephen J. Covey

In the previous lesson, we introduced research presented by the National Scientific Council on the Developing Child (2015) that identified the presence of one stable relationship as a positive factor in promoting adaptability in the face of significant adversity. The Council's work includes additional elements that counterbalance the negative effects of adverse experiences, including, but not limited to

▶ Helping children build a sense of mastery over their life circumstances. Those who believe in their own capacity to overcome hardships and guide their own destiny are far more likely to adapt positively to adversity.

> The supportive context of affirming faith or cultural traditions. Children who are solidly grounded within such traditions are more likely to respond effectively when challenged by a major stressor or a severely disruptive experience. (p. 5)

Furthermore, research has shown that empathy and emotional intelligence are two predictive factors associated with a positive adaptive process (Xing et al., 2023). Thus, this lesson focuses on the way in which we as educators can ignite hope in the lives of our students by engaging in an authentic quest to understand who they are, what they've experienced, and how they learn. Once we do this, we build the foundation for helping learners cultivate skills, courage, and confidence in response to adverse conditions. In the process, we develop our own emotional intelligence and empathic response, which nourishes our well-being and fosters the social, emotional, and academic growth of our students.

PROMPTS TO PONDER

- What does the term *seek to understand* mean to you?
- How might authentically seeking to understand your colleagues, students, or their families impact your ability to respond to challenging life or work situations?
- What might it look like to practice courageous vulnerability in your effort to understand another's lived experience?
- How might seeking to understand the story behind a student who appears disengaged in school contribute to their academic, social, or emotional growth?

IGNITE!

Seeking to understand is our third lesson, and it can begin with the simple act of *acknowledging* that the ways which we, educators and students alike, encounter life's adversities are different. Our lived experiences of the same situation can contribute to assumptions and judgments about people. An effective way to counteract our assumptions is to learn more about the lived experiences of others. In doing so, we acknowledge that there is a story behind every student (and every adult, for that matter). Each person is in a particular boat because of their back story. As educators, we ignite hope when we pursue intentional change by genuinely seeking to understand our students, their families, and our colleagues. This hope stems from the reality that, as we seek to understand not only our students but also their customs, ways, and cultural traditions, we reveal that we sincerely care. It is only after they know we care, as Theodore Roosevelt reminds us, that they will begin to care how much we know. This is essential because our knowledge can help our students "build a sense of mastery over their life circumstances," ultimately elevating their adversity quotient (National Scientific Council on the Developing Child, 2015). We initiate this search for understanding by having a human mindframe.

A human mindframe focuses first and foremost on the person. This perspective promotes the idea that every student within our school community deserves to be recognized for who they are as people. From the moment we walk in the door to school in the morning, *every* child we encounter deserves our consideration. This includes *all* students. All does *not* refer *only* to the students who are ready and willing—who come to class prepared, engage eagerly, and have consistent attendance. *All* includes the ones who haven't done their homework or sit listlessly in the classroom; the ones who spend most of the time in the office for disciplinary reasons; the ones who come to school rarely; the ones who are disconnected from *us* but compulsively connected to their phones. Additionally, a human mindframe recognizes *every* student, regardless of ethnicity, race, socioeconomic status, sexual orientation, gender identity, or physical, emotional, or learning challenges. A human mindframe reminds us that we have a responsibility to engage in equitable practices to optimize the learning environment for *all*.

Data can inform our capacity to better understand our students and to recognize the disparities in discipline that exist in our educational systems. Statistics demonstrate disproportionality across our nation. According to the ACLU, "A fundamental fact, often ignored, is that a student's race has a substantial impact on how the student experiences education, including the opportunities they are likely to be provided or denied" (Jordan, 2023). For example, according to the U.S. Department of Education, the 2020–2021 Civil Rights Data Collection documented that "Black boys were nearly two times more likely to receive an out-of-school suspension or expulsion than White boys," and "Black girls were nearly two times more likely to receive one or more in-school suspensions, one or more out-of-school suspensions, and expulsions than White girls" (Office for Civil Rights, 2023, p. 7). Furthermore, a Brookings report stated that students of color are disproportionately overrepresented, in general, among children with disabilities, with Black students being 40 percent more likely and Native American students 70 percent more likely than their peers to be identified as having disabilities. And these students with disabilities are twice as likely to receive at least one out-of-school suspension than their peers without disabilities (Gordon, 2018). Most educators recognize the reality of this data and realize it is a systemic issue that calls for intentional change. Although efforts are taking place to tackle disproportionality, we still have a long way to go. We persevere, however, because increasing our awareness of this data helps us to create conscious change, applying an equitable approach through which students learn, are disciplined, and are provided support.

The reality is that, as a system, our talk about equity and fairness doesn't match our walk. If we are going to talk about equity, we must begin to actually *walk it*! In order to *walk the talk* of equity, we need to acknowledge that we have built-in biases and that our biases affect the way we interact with and react to others. Thus, seeking to understand requires us to examine our own implicit biases and examine the impact such biases may have on our ability to understand, celebrate, and honor the human beings who are our students, our students' families, and our colleagues.

Let's pause for a moment to reflect and contemplate. How might becoming aware of our biases help us to seek to understand? How might seeking to understand help us to be culturally relevant or culturally responsive? How might your answers to these questions ignite hope in the lives of your students and others? Please share your thoughts here:

_____

_____

_____

_____

_____

_____

_____

_____

_____

_____

Thank you for taking a moment to reflect. Our self-reflection empowers us to "change the things we can"—things, perhaps, that we did not recognize before. As we reflect, we expand our empathic capacity and recognize the child behind the assessment data and the human being behind the behavior. As our capacity grows, we also acknowledge that a human being lies behind the most irritating behaviors of our colleagues as well. We can't forget that.

But in the context of our students, think about this: The students we tend to have the most difficult time building relationships with—the ones who tend to be sent to the office and the ones who are victims of bullying or the aggressors of bullying—are often the students who are living in the reality of adversity. Although they may act tough, disrespectful, rude, or apathetic, there are often several underlying factors contributing to these behaviors. In fact, "behavior that comes off as apathetic or rude might actually indicate feelings of hopelessness and despair" (Jensen, 2009). According to the CDC's *Youth at Risk Behavior Survey Data Summary and Trends Report*, there is a consistent upward trend of students who have experienced persistent feelings of sadness or hopelessness, with over 40 percent of Hispanic students, 46 percent of female students, and 66 percent of students who identify as LGBTQ+ reporting these feelings in 2019. How do we ignite hope for these students? We engage our empathy, think about our biases, and strive to look beyond their behavior to glimpse the true story behind our students.

One way in which to expand our empathic response is to ask ourselves, What are our students carrying in their invisible backpacks? Make no mistake; they all wear them, and the truth of the matter is, so do we. Our backpacks are full of our life experiences. These metaphoric backpacks carry our triumphs and our tragedies, our celebrations, and our challenges. Some of our backpacks are a bit lighter because we may have more stability, opportunity, and strategies to confront stress, trials, or tragedies when they arise. But some of our students' bags (and our colleagues' too) might be heavy with trauma or experiences beyond our imagination. Issues such as homelessness, addiction, anxiety or mental illness, loss of income, sexual abuse, or incarcerated family members are but a few of the burdens that our students carry to school with them daily. When a student is chronically absent or doesn't engage in a lesson, we cannot assume that we know the reason; we need to seek to understand the reason—the story behind the action.

Consider a time in your vocation in which you made assumptions about a student. Please reflect on the experience and what you learned from that specific situation. Is it possible the outcome could have been more positive had you sought to understand the behavior first, to intentionally see the story behind the student? Please reflect upon and process these questions here:

_____

_____

_____

_____

_____

_____

_____

_____

_____

_____

As educators, we can foster educational environments in which all students can thrive. If we are attentive to the root causes of the challenges our students encounter and seek to understand the effect such root causes have on them and on their learning, we can support their development and growth. Often, educators express a concern that they do not know where to start. Actually, it is quite simple: Start with the child, not the content. Start with authentic curiosity, asking open-ended questions in a desire to learn more about the story behind the student. We can also begin by learning about experiences that may not be a part of our own life story, such as historical oppression, racial biases, or situational and generational poverty. Our students, especially those with a lower adversity quotient, need for us to see them for who they are and what they've been through and meet them there in the midst of their often-chaotic worlds. Our authentic quest to know them better will also help us to tap into their strengths. So often, it is a student's behavior that draws our attention. However, the more we get to know them, the more adept we will become at identifying specific traits, lived experiences, or skills that they already possess. When we call out these strengths, we empower our students to engage in their own learning experience, and we buoy their ability to respond in a productive way to life's challenges.

As educators, we use a strengths-based approach when we frame what a young person can do, not solely focus on what they can't do. Wisconsin's Department of Public Education (n.d.) exemplifies the importance of this approach by identifying six domains as Principles for Teaching and Learning within their academic standards. Domain 5, specifically, reads: "Students bring strengths and experiences to learning." Further, they provide the following context for this domain: "Every student learns. Although no two students come to school with the same culture, learning strengths, background knowledge, or experiences, and no two students learn in exactly the same way, every student's unique personal history enriches classrooms, schools, and the community. This diversity is our greatest education asset."

Reflect on the opportunities you create within your instructional setting to identify and leverage student strengths. Do you provide opportunities for analytic, creative, *and* practical thinking? Do you include sensory components into your lesson design? What about opportunities that foster student collaboration and student agency (think back to Lesson One)? Perhaps you provide opportunities for students to identify their strengths through an inventory survey or celebrate their strengths through individual or public recognition. Share instructional practices or other ways in which you identify, leverage, or celebrate student strengths. Then, reflect on any observed positive impact from such practice.

I identify, leverage, and/or celebrate student strengths in these ways:

_____

_____

_____

_____

_____

I notice the following positive impact when I use a strength-based approach:

_____

_____

_____

_____

_____

Students with a low adversity quotient tend to be unaware of their strengths. When we reframe for strengths or provide opportunities to identify, celebrate, or leverage strengths, we ignite tangible hope for our students. Furthermore, when we employ a human mindframe, engage in equitable practices, show empathy, and give compassion to our students and ourselves, we demonstrate an authentic quest to understand.

IGNITE INTENTION

Please consider one way in which you will choose to ignite hope by seeking to understand one student or group of students with whom you have made assumptions or neglected to learn about or honor their lived experiences.

Student's first name, group identifier, or initial/s:_____

I will seek to better understand this student by (thinking, saying, being, or doing . . .):

_____

_____

_____

_____

_____

NOURISH!

According to Oxford Languages, to nourish is to provide with the food or other substances necessary for growth, health, and good condition. In the realm of who we are as educators, such substances necessary to nurture our well-being and support the well-being of those with whom we interact include our aptitude for practicing vulnerability, empathy, and listening. Some believe that being vulnerable equates to being weak. We disagree. Allowing oneself to be vulnerable can be an act of courage, a willingness to look within, a step toward serenity or intentional change. Vulnerability calls for us to ask, "Why do we think, say, or do the things we do? What is our lived experience that causes us to be defensive, impatient, or intolerant?" Reflecting authentically in this way helps us to identify our own strengths and recognize areas of our lives in which we might grow. For example, Doug keeps a failure résumé. This résumé includes epic fails and the impact that they have had on him. An early entry is a comment from a professor during his master's degree program. On the front page of his thesis, the professor simply wrote, "Start over." As painful as this was, not to mention how inappropriate the feedback was, the failure taught Doug to carefully consider feedback and the impact that it has on the receiver.

Being empathetic can nurture selflessness, kindness, and understanding. These traits sustain our well-being in that they suppress negativity, judgment, and angst, which in turn help us to have a more positive attitude and peaceful spirit. Empathy also expands our view of the world around us, providing insight and awareness as we pursue acceptance and consideration for people and experiences that are different from us and ours. As such, being empathetic will help us to nurture stronger relationships and more authentic communication.

Take a moment to consider a time in your life as a student in which someone at school showed you empathy. What do you remember about that situation? How did you feel prior to the person's empathetic response? How did you feel after? What behaviors do you recall the person demonstrating? What was their demeanor? Tone of voice? Word choice? Please reflect on these questions here:

_____

_____

_____

_____

_____

_____

_____

_____

_____

Enhancing our aptitude for listening also provides nourishment because earnest listening requires that we slow down, take pause, and focus. Heartfelt listening abides by the *less is more* philosophy. Less trying to fix people or situations. More being authentically present as we support others in identifying their own needs or solutions. Listening means less of us telling our own stories and more of us seeking to understand the stories of those we teach or lead. The actual practice of active listening requires intentionality and presence of mind and body. This practice can settle us and foster a sense of peace and calm. Listening nourishes the well-being of others because it is about empathy and active compassion. Doug and Nancy have declared often in their writing and speaking that a fundamental aspect of respect and dignity is the ability to listen and communicate that you have listened.

Consider what listening looks like when you engage with a student or colleague who is sharing a concern with you. How does your body language appear? What words do you use or what words or phrases do you avoid? How does the student or colleague know you are listening based on your way of being, response, or lack thereof? Please share your reflections:

_____

_____

_____

_____

_____

_____

_____

_____

Listening can also positively influence belonging, which in turn nourishes well-being. It's easier to build a sense of belonging in the classroom with students who already possess the prosocial skills and academic prowess that we equate with school success. But what about those who don't? Being an educator means accepting a truth: Young people will not always be their best. How can we be there for them and accept them when they are not their best selves? We can begin by seeking to understand through modeling active listening while we seek to understand by being intentionally present.

These same techniques work well with colleagues who are processing something that they find challenging. Our instinct to take care of another person often starts with listening to their concerns. We may, or may not, have the same concerns or experiences as the other person. But listening to them can help them feel heard and perhaps even help resolve the issue. The key, though, is to avoid getting pulled into their emotions. Whether talking with a young person who is struggling or a colleague who is facing a dilemma, consider your active listening skills and identify areas that you may need to attend to.

- Give the person your full and undivided attention and eliminate environmental distractions. This may include changing the setting for the conversation.

- Avoid thinking about what you're going to say next. The opposite of speaking isn't waiting to speak again. It's listening.

- Identify key words or phrases and repeat them, but don't comment on them. In doing so, you demonstrate that you are attuned to the speaker.

- Ask open-ended questions that invite them to elaborate or speculate. "When you say that you're crushed by what happened, what do you mean? What did that feel like when it happened, and how is it feeling now?"

- When it is necessary for you to comment, use "I" statements. "What I think I am understanding is . . ." invites the person to acknowledge or clarify what feelings they are experiencing.

- Don't interrupt.

Consider the various content, behaviors, and/or strategies discussed in this section. Please take a moment to use the template on the following page to create a goal for yourself specific to one new behavior for seeking to understand that will nourish your own well-being or that of your colleagues or students.

Goal Statement:

SMART Goal Checklist: ☐ Specific ☐ Measurable ☐ Attainable
☐ Relevant ☐ Time-Bound

Why is this goal important?

How does this goal connect with my why?

What is my past experience or performance with this goal?

What are the benefits of my goal? What are the potential
challenges or barriers?

How will I, or what skills/resources do I need, to measure, review,
refine, and achieve my goal?

Action Steps:

1.

2.

3.

Start Date: | Review and Refine Date/s: | Completion Date:

ENGAGE!

When we seek to understand our students, we are more prepared to affirm their customs, faith, or cultural traditions. Remember that "children who are solidly grounded within such traditions are more likely to respond effectively when challenged by a major stressor or a severely disruptive experience" (National Scientific Council on the Developing Child, 2015). We have the ability to engage our students and their families by behaving in a manner that acknowledges that customs, cultures, and ways of being for our students may be different from ours. Culturally aware educators understand that different is simply different, not less. We demonstrate that we are pursuing equity and seeking to understand all members of our school community when we acknowledge our own personal biases, demonstrating acceptance of and appreciation for differences. In an interview with Dr. Greta Peay from Infinity: Diversity Matters, she reminds us that seeking to understand requires us to be culturally responsive and attune to various learning styles. Dr. Peay suggests,

> Teachers who seek to understand discover how their students learn and therefore can guide them and lead them to grow in their learning. Educators who know their students as unique individuals can help them to navigate the often confusing and anxiety-filled lives that they lead. This lens and skill set, however, will require educators to be aware of their own personal bias. . . . Culturally responsive educators are aware and are constantly building relationships with their students and their families. They understand the importance of students feeling respected, valued, and seen for who they are. Educators have the unique power to impact the lives

of their learners. Culturally responsive educators make use of thoughtful, inclusive instruction to enhance the learning environment for their students that lasts far beyond their time in the classroom.

As we suggested in the previous section, our authentic quest for understanding can foster a sense of belonging that in turn cultivates an instructional environment in which students are more willing to take risks, work with others, and engage in their own learning. Thus, we will focus on belonging as we explore 11 dimensions that contribute to belonging and teacher practices that foster these dimensions.

ELEVEN DIMENSIONS OF BELONGING IN SCHOOLS

Evidence demonstrates that when students at the university level experience a sense of belonging in certain contexts, it can result in improved academic outcomes, continued enrollment, and protective mental health factors (MIT Teaching + Learning Lab, n.d.). Likewise, multiple data sources suggest a sense of belonging among elementary and secondary students promotes prosocial behavior, academic engagement, improved attendance, and decreased discipline referrals. But what does it mean to belong? Stanford researcher Geoff Cohen proposes the following: "Belonging is the feeling that we're part of a larger group that values, respects, and cares for us—and to which we feel we have something to contribute" (Cohen, 2022, p. 5). There are several important aspects of this definition. It's a feeling. In other words, we know it when we experience it. Belonging involves a larger group, and that group exhibits certain behaviors toward us. We experience being valued, respected, and cared for. And the kicker in this definition is that belonging includes a feeling that we have something to contribute to the group. Each part of this definition is important for educators to consider as they create spaces where students know that they belong.

We have adapted and adopted the 11 dimensions of belonging (Carter, 2021). Remember, when students and staff know that they belong, their performance is enhanced, and they are happier to be at school.

1. *Welcome*: The way we are greeted each time we meet

2. *Invited*: Being asked to be part of activities and events

3. *Present*: Who is in attendance and fully present

4. *Known*: The depth to which we know others and their strengths

5. *Accepted*: Ways we are recognized and celebrated as a member of the group

6. *Involved*: How we participate actively and intentionally with a group

7. *Heard*: Seeking the perspectives of others and actively listening when they share

8. *Supported*: Recognition of our uniqueness and systems to aid our participation

9. *Befriended*: Being friendly and encouraging and facilitating friendships

10. *Needed*: Contributing to others and recognizing the value of those contributions

11. *Loved*: Agape, or the selfless, unconditional love that conveys compassion and empathy

The following menu includes a list of each of the dimensions of belonging that Carter identified. We include sample indicators of each dimension for students and staff. You are encouraged to add your own indicators.

Menu of Practices That Foster Belonging

Use the checklist to reflect on your current practices as they relate to creating opportunities for connection by establishing (or reestablishing) relationships with students.

Use the following reflection scale:

1: I consistently create opportunities for this to occur in my instructional setting.

2: I sometimes create opportunities for this to occur in my instructional setting.

3: I rarely or never create opportunities for this to occur in my instructional setting.

Factor	Indicators for Students	1	2	3	Indicators for Staff	1	2	3
Welcomed	Greeting students by name	☐	☐	☐	Greeting colleagues by name	☐	☐	☐
	Showing enthusiasm for students' return to class each day	☐	☐	☐	Asking authentic questions	☐	☐	☐
					Engaging in authentic conversations	☐	☐	☐
Invited	Students asking peers to play	☐	☐	☐	Sending invites for meetings and learning events	☐	☐	☐
	Staff extending invitations for extracurricular events and clubs	☐	☐	☐	Extending invitations for other professional opportunities (advising, club sponsorship)	☐	☐	☐
	Educators modeling inviting behavior	☐	☐	☐		☐	☐	☐

(Continued)

(Continued)

Factor	Indicators for Students	1	2	3	Indicators for Staff	1	2	3
Present	Staff fostering strong student attendance rates	☐	☐	☐	Strong staff attendance rates	☐	☐	☐
	Students participating in class activities	☐	☐	☐	Participating in team meetings and learning activities	☐	☐	☐
Known	Pronouncing names correctly	☐	☐	☐	Addressing biased and stereotyped language	☐	☐	☐
	Strong teacher-student relationships	☐	☐	☐	Emotional intelligence and positive dialogues	☐	☐	☐
	Focusing on strengths	☐	☐	☐		☐	☐	☐
Accepted	Positive body language and nonverbal messages from teachers and peers	☐	☐	☐	Positive body language and nonverbal messages toward colleagues	☐	☐	☐
	Symbols of respect for all student groups	☐	☐	☐	Inclusive beliefs and actions about students, staff, and community	☐	☐	☐
	Culturally sustaining instructional materials	☐	☐	☐		☐	☐	☐

Factor	Indicators for Students	1	2	3	Indicators for Staff	1	2	3
Involved	Opportunities for collaborative learning	☐	☐	☐	Collaborating with colleagues in team meetings	☐	☐	☐
	Students and teachers using academic language	☐	☐	☐	Contributing to tasks required to operate the school	☐	☐	☐
	Students setting goals for their learning	☐	☐	☐		☐	☐	☐
Heard	Active listening (and teachers talking less)	☐	☐	☐	Staff involvement in decisions	☐	☐	☐
	Soliciting feedback from students	☐	☐	☐	Distributed leadership	☐	☐	☐
	Student choice and decision-making in how they demonstrate understanding	☐	☐	☐	Leaders engaged in dialogue, not monologue	☐	☐	☐
Supported	Strong instructional scaffolds in place	☐	☐	☐	Professional learning is practical and responsive to staff needs and interests	☐	☐	☐
	Sophisticated tiers of support (RTI/MTSS)	☐	☐	☐	Peer coaching and feedback	☐	☐	☐
	Modeling and demonstrating, not just telling information	☐	☐	☐	Restorative conversations	☐	☐	☐

(Continued)

(Continued)

Factor	Indicators for Students	1	2	3	Indicators for Staff	1	2	3
Befriended	Structured opportunities for students to interact with a wide range of peers	☐	☐	☐	Social opportunities for staff to interact	☐	☐	☐
	Integrated peer relationship development in the curriculum	☐	☐	☐	Collegial and friendly interactions in hallways, restrooms, and classrooms	☐	☐	☐
Needed	Students helping each other	☐	☐	☐	Peer coaching	☐	☐	☐
	Peer tutoring	☐	☐	☐	Peer-to-peer conversations	☐	☐	☐
	Students collaborating with peers	☐	☐	☐	Sharing resources and ideas	☐	☐	☐
Loved	Showing patience, effort, and unity	☐	☐	☐	Making statements of empathy	☐	☐	☐
	Providing comfort to students	☐	☐	☐	Offering words of grace and forgiveness	☐	☐	☐
	Building meaningful relationships	☐	☐	☐		☐	☐	☐

Source: Adapted from Fisher, D., & Frey, N. (2024). What does it mean to belong? *Educational Leadership, 81*(5), 80-81.

ENGAGE EXTENSION

Please consider your responses to the Menu of Practices That Foster Belonging and respond to the following prompts.

My current practices reflect strengths in the following areas:

_____

_____

_____

_____

_____

I notice that I rarely, if ever, create opportunities for (choose one for which you checked "3" or one suggestion from _____ content):

_____

_____

_____

_____

_____

I will begin providing opportunities to practice what I noticed above by (specifically doing what?):

_____

_____

_____

_____

_____

LESSON REFLECTION

As you have done in the previous lessons, please take a moment to consider the specific actions noted in the following table that foster our ability to seek to understand others and ourselves during adverse experiences. At the same time, contemplate specific actions that can derail our efforts to practice empathy, take perspective, or be curious when we experience situations that cause us to feel overwhelmed, frustrated, helpless, or hopeless. Identify any actions that resonate with you, validate you, or cause you to question why you do what you do. Then, fill in the blank spaces with acts or behaviors specific to your way of being that cultivate empathic response and foster compassion, respect, and equity, as well as some in the opposing column that contribute to derailing a quest for authentic understanding.

Actions That Foster Understanding of Others	Actions That Derail Understanding of Others

Please consider the *Ignite, Nourish*, and *Engage* sections of this lesson. Use the following space to reflect upon one intentional mindset and/or behavior you would like to *stop, start,* and *continue* in the sphere of seeking to understand your students, colleagues, or yourself. Choose one to *stop* because, upon reflection, you realize your thought, words, or behavior limit your understanding of the lived experiences of others. Choose one mindset or behavior you would like to *start* promoting your ability to have a human mindframe, engage in empathetic listening, equitable practices, and compassionate action, or be more open-minded and -hearted. Finally, choose one mindset or behavior you realize you practice well and want to *continue.*

Please personalize your answers here.

STOP:

_____

_____

_____

_____

_____

START:

_____

_____

_____

_____

_____

CONTINUE:

_____

_____

_____

_____

_____

Seeking to understand is paramount in elevating the adversity quotient. The quest provides perspective, opens the door to empathy, and promotes endurance. Powerful strategies such as providing empathetic feedback promote agency and self-efficacy and contribute to one's ability to persevere through hardship. Ultimately, as we seek to understand, we meet our students right where they are, and ourselves, reaffirming that none of us is alone and that we can all increase our ability to thrive through adversity.

 CORE CONNECTION

Endurance is our ability to persist through difficult times and face challenges. This helps us rebound from problems and maintain a positive attitude even when circumstances are trying (Stoltz, 1997).

Seeking to understand fosters endurance. Perseverance through difficult times is more challenging when we believe that no one knows or understands what we are going through. People are more able to endure amid significant adversity when those around them are open-minded, empathetic, and supportive. In our pursuit of understanding, we validate that even in the midst of challenge we believe in our students and their capacity to surmount hardships and prevail in the face of adversity.

4

LEAD WITH LOVE

We know from a great deal of research in neuroscience, biology, developmental and cognitive, that learning and development occur in relationally-rich environments; that loving relationships contribute to thriving while creating a physiological, emotional, and cognitive readiness to learn. We also know from research in history, sociology, and social psychology that social factors such as bias, privilege, and segregation separate us; that these are reinforced by stress and cultural incapacity; and that it is important to build and support the capacity of educators to love as well as teach "other people's children."

—David Osher

We realize that *love* may not be considered the latest evidence-based program or new initiative in education, but as Osher suggests, it is vital that we consider the importance of love in the context of student well-being, achievement, and growth. It's also part of what creates a strong sense of belonging.

Let us explain a perspective that supports a common mantra, emphasizing that we must *Maslow before we can Bloom*. We were all taught Maslow's hierarchy of needs (as well as Bloom's Taxonomy of Educational Objectives) in college, and we value its premise. Maslow suggested that lower levels of need must be met, such as physiological and safety, before the respective higher levels of need, specifically the need for love, acceptance, and belonging, can be realized. In the context of individuals living in the reality of substantial adverse conditions, Maslow's motivational theory is particularly significant. For some students, school is the one place in which their physiological or safety needs are sure to be met. There are students walking in the hallways of our schools for whom school is potentially the only place they are assured a roof over their heads, food in their bellies, and in some cases, even, clothes on their backs.

In fact, some schools offer a washer and dryer for students to use. Some families simply don't have the means to provide for school clothes or clean laundry. By providing t-shirts for all students and a washer and dryer so they can choose to launder their clothes at school, schools can do more than provide an avenue to assure our students' physiological and safety needs are being met. They are operating on a foundation of love.

 PROMPTS TO PONDER

- When you think of "leading with love" within the realm of your vocational practice, what is the first thing that comes to your mind?

- As an educator, how might coming from a place of love in the way in which you respond to a difficult situation foster a more positive or productive outcome?

- How might leading with love contribute to improved student engagement or academic growth?
- How might you model leading with love, especially when a student or staff member is experiencing adversity?

IGNITE!

Regardless of the role we serve as an educator, we don't have to be labeled an educational leader to lead with love. We all can *choose* to be leaders—of our own lives and of our own sphere of influence. Cornel West wisely reminds us, "You can't lead the people, if you don't love the people" (@CornelWest, 2013). When we choose to approach our students and our colleagues from a place of love, then with empathy and encouragement, we foster acceptance, trust, self-efficacy, and responsiveness to high expectations and accountability. Choosing to lead with love means we engage with our students and all members of our school community in a way that goes beyond the responsibilities associated with our job descriptions. We willingly consider the needs of the whole child to enhance a student's school experience, and we find ways to reach beyond meeting safety and physiological needs to support and encourage our students, their families, and our colleagues. In the face of significant adversity, interacting with one who approaches situations through the lens of love can bring hope to what may seem to be a hopeless, impossible situation. Ultimately, by leading with love we can support one's journey toward Maslow's self-actualization or, educationally speaking, academic and personal success. The *Start With the Heart* hierarchy image assumes safety and physiological needs are met in the school setting, thus the foundation from which we operate is love.

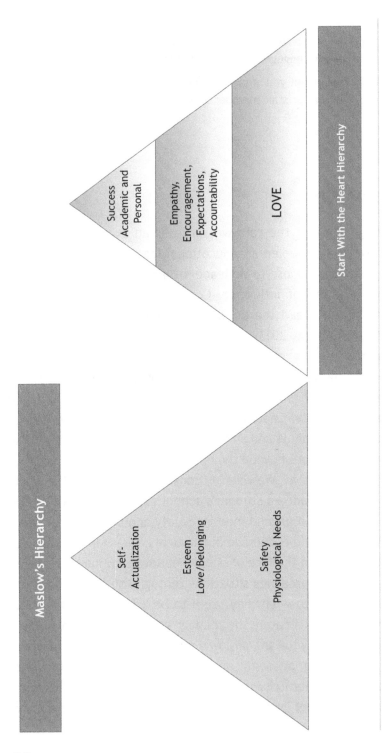

Maslow's Hierarchy

Self-Actualization

Esteem
Love/Belonging

Safety
Physiological Needs

Start With the Heart Hierarchy

Success
Academic and Personal

Empathy,
Encouragement,
Expectations,
Accountability

LOVE

Choosing to *lead* with love—to come from a place of love in all that we are and all that we do—is critical today. Reflect on the idea of invisible backpacks we explored as a consideration for seeking to understand. People carrying burdens may do things or say things that we don't agree with or understand. Before we jump to conclusions or cast judgments, let's practice patience, tolerance, mercy, and forgiveness. In doing so, we lead from a place of love, respect, and understanding. Consider the antithesis. If we are not stepping out or leaning in with love, then what? Typically, we respond, or more often react, from a place of fear. Fear can breed assumption, pessimism, and divisiveness. Consider a situation from your personal or professional life in which the outcome was negative. Ask yourself, did I approach the situation or the person with love or fear? As with other intentional behaviors we have discussed, this type of self-reflection may require you to practice courageous vulnerability, but in doing so, your answer may reveal that revisiting the situation from a place of love may result in a more positive outcome.

Will you reflect here on an experience you had when you were a student in which an educator led with love in a way that positively influenced your life and/or your learning? How did this educator's approach impact you at that time? What still stands out?

_____

_____

_____

_____

_____

_____

_____

_____

_____

How about as an educator yourself? Was there a moment in your vocational career when it may not have been your first inclination to lead with love, but you did so anyway? What did the experience look like? What did it feel like? Feel free to use this space to reflect on these questions:

_____

_____

_____

_____

_____

_____

_____

_____

_____

Leading with love is not about being warm and fuzzy. It is about intentional consideration of the way in which we approach people and situations. Coming from a place of love with our students and their families often means setting high expectations or boundaries and then providing support as needed so that objectives or goals can be met. Leading with love says, *I trust that you are capable and that you can meet set goals or expectations, so I'm setting the bar high. I believe in you. I care about you and your success.* When we lead with love, people feel encouraged, opportunities are expanded, and hope is ignited!

IGNITE INTENTION

Please consider one way in which you will choose to ignite hope by leading with love in the way you approach a specific situation or interact with one student or group of students with whom you have made assumptions or neglected to learn about or honor their lived experiences.

Situation: _____ or student's first name or initial: _____

I will intentionally lead with love in this situation or with this student/group by (thinking, saying, being, or doing . . .):

_____

_____

_____

_____

_____

NOURISH!

Think back to the first lesson: *Be Intentional.* Leading with love requires being intentional about the little things, especially in the face of adversity when we tend to feel overwhelmed or when our lives seem out of our control. Intentionally seeking joy, for instance, is a small step we can take from a place of love that can be nourishing to mind, body, and soul. As much as we have all faced adversity at different seasons in our lives, we have also experienced people, places, or experiences that cause us to feel joyful. Take a moment to consider, what brings you joy? Is it a person or a group of people who make your heart smile? Does joy greet you through an experience or activity in which you engage? Or might it be a specific place, such as the mountains or the ocean, where you find joy? Take a moment to reflect on that which brings you joy:

_____

_____

_____

_____

_____

_____

_____

_____

_____

It may seem implausible that taking charge of our own lives by focusing on what brings us joy might lift us in the face of adversity, but the fact of that matter is that it can, and it does. Think just for a moment about how you feel in this instant after writing about what brings you joy in comparison to before your self-reflection. Likely, you feel a bit lighter; perhaps you smiled when writing; maybe your focus is more positive. Seeking joy is one of the little things that, as John Wooden says, can make a big impact, because leading with love not only allows us to seek joy, but to provide opportunities for others to experience joy through compassionate action.

Earlier in this lesson, we addressed setting high expectations and firm boundaries as a way to ignite hope for our students; however, leading with love in this way does not only apply to those with whom we are working. We nourish our own well-being when we set boundaries for ourselves, have high expectations for our health, and practice being accountable. Setting boundaries seems a natural fit in the context of protecting our well-being. Educators are notorious for taking on too much; thus, cultivating the courage to say "no" when asked to do one more thing, join one more committee, or take one more meeting can be empowering. Choosing to leave school in time to prioritize family responsibilities or to carve out quality time with friends is a boundary that can safeguard our mental, emotional, and physical health. Personal boundaries are important—especially for educators, because most of us innately have a servant's heart. It is second nature for us to be there for others—so much so that we unintentionally neglect our own needs or those of our family. It is okay to say no; believe us—the world will not fall apart. And you may even find that you are more at peace, happier, and more productive.

Setting high expectations for our health is another way in which we can lead with love in our lives. As much as we may not feel as if we have time, we can choose to be cognizant of the type of food we put in our bodies. If we need to eat to survive (back to Maslow's hierarchy of needs), why not choose to eat well? God grant me the serenity to accept the things I cannot change, the courage to change the things I can, and the wisdom to know the difference. Avoiding fast food is something over which we have control. Honoring our bodies with nutrient-dense foods, choosing to set a goal for steps per day, or increasing our activity in a specific way is within our realm to change and will nurture our well-being.

Accountability, on the other hand, doesn't seem a natural behavior associated with nourishing our well-being. So let us connect the dots. Being accountable can nurture our well-being in two ways. First, consider this. Have you ever made a choice about which you have felt guilty? Have you said something that you knew hurt someone's feelings, or have you acted in a way that negatively impacted another? Perhaps you engaged in gossip, placed blame, or cast judgment. We remind you again that we are all human, and none of us is perfect. However, we all possess the ability to make things right when we make a poor choice. You may be wondering what this has to do with nourishing our well-being. Consider that guilt is heavy. It takes courage to own our missteps, to seek sincere forgiveness, but it will lighten our load. More than that, it is an act of leadership and of love because it demonstrates consideration for another's feelings, and it is a skill that helps us to encounter adverse situations with a degree of control, which ultimately can elevate our own adversity quotient while modeling an effective skill for others. Secondly, being accountable calls for us to take ownership of our choices and our future. It reminds us that it is within our power to set goals for ourselves, to be solution-oriented instead of problem-focused, and to recognize and leverage our strengths while being cognizant of skills and behaviors we might improve. When we are accountable to ourselves, we are trustworthy, reliable, and self-reflective—all qualities that nurture our social emotional well-being.

Finally, leading with love must begin within. We cannot address the concept of leading with love without considering self-love. So many of us are hard on ourselves. We often tell ourselves stories based on our past experiences that may result in thoughts such as, *I'm not good enough. No one cares what I think.* And *if I ask for help, I'll look incompetent.* These thoughts or stories are judgmental and lacking in acceptance of ourselves. Leading with love in an effort to make a positive impact in the lives of others will be meaningless if we do not first love ourselves. This act looks different for different people. For some of us, it is a matter of being patient with ourselves and giving ourselves grace. We ask you to consider, are you as kind to yourself as you are to a friend? It is not unusual for people to be much harder on themselves than they are on friends, family, or those they see in need of support. When we practice self-love by appreciating, respecting, and giving grace to ourselves, we are better prepared to love and care for others.

Self-love can also mean practicing courageous vulnerability by reaching out to others because it is difficult to admit when we are uncertain, lonely, or sad. Yet people typically want to be there for one another, and if we don't communicate our needs, those who care for us cannot offer support or guidance. To take it a step further, loving ourselves can look like asking for help. This life was not meant to be lived in isolation. The fact that we all have different strengths, character traits, and personalities is a blessing that can contribute to the greater good. If only we were all to rely on each other just a little bit more!

Please consider the last few paragraphs. Is there one idea or "aha" that resonates with you? Is there one specific action you can take to lead with love in a way that nourishes your well-being? Feel free to use this space to share your thoughts:

_____

_____

_____

_____

_____

_____

_____

_____

_____

NOURISH NOW

People with an elevated ability to respond to adversity with perseverance, adaptability, and open-mindedness are likely to lead with love, as opposed to leading with fear, judgment, anger, or rigidity. Please consider the way in which you lead with love in your own life or in the way in which you respond to situations or interact with others. Might there be one goal you can set for yourself that would nourish your well-being or that of those with whom you interact? Please use the following template to enhance your ability.

Goal Statement:

SMART Goal Checklist: ☐ Specific ☐ Measurable ☐ Attainable
☐ Relevant ☐ Time-Bound

Why is this goal important?

How does this goal connect with my why?

What is my past experience or performance with this goal?

What are the benefits of my goal? What are the potential challenges or barriers?

How will I, or what skills/resources do I need, to measure, review, refine, and achieve my goal?

Action Steps:
1.
2.
3.

Start Date:

Review and Refine Date/s:

Completion Date:

ENGAGE!

Leading with love in the ways we interact with our students and colleagues when there is conflict or interpersonal challenges requires that we restore any harm that has occurred. Using restorative approaches, teams of educators are helping students recognize the harm that they have caused and are providing opportunities for students to make amends and learn from their mistakes. A randomized study of restorative practices at the middle school level found that it was an effective vehicle for positive youth development (Acosta et al., 2019).

Schools do not become restorative overnight. In fact, it takes dedication, honest conversations, and effort to change the culture of a school. And it starts with helping teachers gain clarity on their beliefs about justice. We like to begin professional development sessions on restorative practices with the following lines, each revealed one at a time:

➤ *When we encounter a student who cannot read, we teach that student to read.*

➤ *When we encounter a student who struggles in mathematics, we teach that student math.*

➤ *When we encounter a student who does not behave, we punish that student.*

For many, this prompts cognitive dissonance and opens a discussion about our collective purpose for becoming educators. Most participants report that they dedicated their professional lives to the development of children and youth. Accordingly, we should teach prosocial behaviors rather than simply punish students who do not yet know how to behave. In fact, the research on multitiered system of supports (MTSS) frameworks suggests that on average 80 percent of restorative practices should be universal (available to *all* students), proactive, relational practices that build community and trust while teaching expected behaviors. Such practices are foundational to creating a school culture in which we engage and interact with one another from a place of love and empathy as opposed to judgment or fear. Thus, we emphasize five key concepts to support creating prosocial restorative practices in our classrooms and across all aspects of our school community.

FIVE PROACTIVE CONCEPTS TO FOSTER A RESTORATIVE CULTURE

1. **Restorative language:** The language we use can foster inclusivity, build agency, and honor identity. Use affective language and open-ended questions to engage in reflective and relevant conversations. Intentional word choice can promote positive outcomes. For example, "Can you tell me more about . . ." instead of "Why did you . . ." fosters authentic conversation and decreases defensiveness.

2. **Greeting rituals:** Greeting every student, every day, using their name and offering a handshake or high five, a comment, or a compliment is foundational for creating a restorative culture. Students (and teachers too) enter classrooms in a dysregulated state. A restorative ritual can reset, build community, and engage students. Most importantly, each student steps into the classroom knowing they are valued and belong.

3. **Community investment:** *Nothing about us without us.* This is a phrase often used in restorative communities that has its origin in Central European political traditions and South African disability activism. It is an essential concept in education because a fundamental hypothesis of restorative practices is that "people are happier, more cooperative and productive, and more likely to make positive changes in their behavior when those in authority do things *with* them, rather than *to* them or *for* them" (Wachtel, 2016, p. 6). Educational leaders, teachers, and school staff traditionally operate by telling students what

to do or by making decisions *for* them. We build capacity as a community when the insight and concerns of the people impacted by a decision are heard and valued.

4. **Restorative circles:** Restorative circles create community, build trust, and provide an opportunity for all students to be seen and heard. Teachers or circle keepers can set the tone and the topic for the circle. Circles can be used to get to know one another, to practice active listening, to engage in academic learning, and to seek solutions or resolutions. Agreements are set and reviewed for expected circle behavior, including the use of a talking piece to ensure equity of sharing and active listening. Under proper circumstances with trained facilitators, circles can be used to repair harm, restore relationships, and determine meaningful resolution, consequence, and/or reintegration.

5. **Impromptu conversations:** Restorative conversations can be used to teach and support prosocial behavior or address academic or behavioral concerns. Using restorative language, adults and students can engage in productive conversations in which emotions are identified, accountability is practiced, and expected or desired behaviors are determined or taught. Like circles, impromptu conversations are generally a proactive restorative approach. Substantial behavior issues or conflict causing significant harm may require a responsive conversation in the form of a restorative conference led by an adult who is trained in restorative justice practices. This is imperative because if responsive restorative practices are not handled with care and expertise, they can ultimately cause additional harm.

Please reflect on the five proactive concepts that foster a restorative culture and respond to the following prompts. Are there any concepts in which you, or your school community, already engage? If so, what does it look like in your realm of influence? If not, are there any concepts that you would be willing to put into practice consistently for at least two weeks? Can you describe what you can imagine it looking like, and can you determine at least one expected outcome?

_____

_____

_____

_____

_____

_____

_____

_____

_____

We appreciate your reflection and acknowledge that emphasizing proactive, prosocial concepts and practices does not negate the need for responsive restorative practices. We acknowledge that in life, and in education, when relationships exist, harm can occur, requiring the need to repair and restore. As such, we must explore restorative justice in education.

We mentioned that we begin our professional development sessions by helping educators gain clarity on their beliefs about justice. Next, we focus on the definition of justice. When teams of teachers have different perspectives about justice or if they have not clarified their thinking about justice, they tend to focus on punishments. After all, it is familiar. We ask teachers to think of a time they were harmed, either intentionally or unintentionally, by another human being. Then, we ask them to journal about the following questions:

- How did you feel?
- What questions did you want to ask the offender?
- What else did you want to say to them?
- Who or what could make things right for you?
- What would justice have looked like for you?

Once they have done so, we ask them to share with a partner, reminding them that there is no need to share what happened and that the level of disclosure is completely up to them. Most people do. To debrief this experience, we ask people when the harm occurred (not what it was). The majority recalled events from many years ago. We note that people hold onto events when they are not resolved and when amends have not been made. We also note that the most common response to the question that they would like to ask the offender is "Why me?"

From there, we ask people to consider a time in which they have caused another person harm, either intentionally or unintentionally. We also tell them that they will not be asked to share this experience and that they don't need to write it down if they don't want. We do ask them to consider the following questions:

- How were you feeling at the time?
- What would you have liked to say to the victim?
- Who or what would have made things right?
- What would justice have looked like for you and for the victim?

The conversation then moves to justice. What does it mean? How do we ensure justice as well as opportunities for individuals to make amends? And how do we restore the relationships that are damaged along the way? For most groups, this is enough for the first session. However, there is an incremental shift in dispositions as educators reconsider the role of justice and making amends in their lives.

From there, we ask people to reflect on their reactions and responses when problems arise. Do they lead with love and recognize the harm? Or do they immediately move to punishment and exclusionary discipline policies?

The menu here includes actions that require reflection on your personal actions when harm has occurred. The Menu of Practices address harm and how people can address the harm that has been caused. Consider each statement and identify your responses.

Menu of Practices That Help Repair Harm

Reflect on how, in your role, you deal with students (or staff) when an incident or issue has arisen. Answer the questions below by marking a check in the column choices of *1, 2,* or *3.* Use the following reflection scale:

1: *Always*

2: *Usually*

3: *Not Often*

Self-Reflection	1	2	3
Do I remain calm during the conversation?	☐	☐	☐
Do I really listen, without interrupting?	☐	☐	☐
Does the student understand why they are having this conversation?	☐	☐	☐
Would the student say I am a good listener?	☐	☐	☐

(Continued)

(Continued)

Self-Reflection	1	2	3
Do I remain calm during the conversation?	☐	☐	☐
Do we explore how the school values apply to the issue?	☐	☐	☐
Does the student understand the harm they've caused, who has been affected, and how?	☐	☐	☐
Do I talk about how the incident affects me?	☐	☐	☐
Do I take responsibility for any part I might have played when things went wrong, acknowledge it, and apologize?	☐	☐	☐
Do I consider the extent to which I have a relationship with this student and how that affects my expectations for our interaction?	☐	☐	☐
If the student apologizes to me, do I accept the apology respectfully?	☐	☐	☐
Do I collaborate with the student to formulate a plan?	☐	☐	☐
Have I, at any stage, asked someone I trust to observe my practice and give me honest feedback?	☐	☐	☐
Do I try to handle most issues or incidents myself?	☐	☐	☐
Do I seek support when issues get tricky for me?	☐	☐	☐
Do I follow the school's systems when looking for more support?	☐	☐	☐
Is the relationship with the student repaired?	☐	☐	☐

Source: Adapted from the New Zealand Ministry of Education (2014).

ENGAGE EXTENSION

Please consider your responses to the Menu of Practices That Help Repair Harm as well as the content related to leading with love and respond to the following prompts.

My current practices reflect strengths in the following areas:

_____

_____

_____

_____

_____

I notice that I rarely, if ever, create opportunities for (choose one for which you checked 3):

_____

_____

_____

_____

_____

I will begin providing opportunities to practice what I noticed above by (specifically doing what?):

_____

_____

_____

_____

_____

LESSON REFLECTION

Throughout this lesson, we have explored strategies and instructional practices that leverage love. Please take a moment to consider the specific actions noted in the following table that foster our ability to lead with love in the way in which we interact with students, their families, and our colleagues. Likewise, consider specific actions that can derail our efforts to respond from a place of love when we experience challenging situations, vocational frustrations, or conflict with colleagues, students, or their families or caregivers. Contemplate those actions that resonate with you, validate you, or cause you to be curious. Then, fill in the blank spaces with acts or behaviors specific to your way of being that lead with love, as well as those that derail your ability to respond from a place of love, specifically in the face of adversity.

Actions That Foster Leading With Love	Actions That Derail Leading With Love

For this final lesson, we ask that you again consider the content, reflections, and strategies from each section. Use the space here to reflect upon one intentional mindset and/or behavior you would like to *stop, start,* and *continue* in the sphere of leading with love in the lives of your students, their families, and your colleagues. Choose one mindset or behavior you would like to *stop* because, upon reflection, you realize it does not come from a place of love. Choose one mindset or behavior you would like to *start* promoting your ability to more authentically practice coming from a place of love in your thoughts, attitudes, and practice. Finally, choose one mindset or behavior you realize you practice well and want to *continue.*

Please personalize your answers here.

STOP:

_____

_____

_____

_____

_____

START:

_____

_____

_____

_____

_____

CONTINUE:

_____

_____

_____

_____

_____

Maya Angelou was a woman who left a significant mark on this world with the way she lived her life. Love seemed to permeate from her every pore. She led with love in the way that she interacted with others and in the way she took care of herself. One of the most enlightening video clips we have ever seen was one in which Maya Angelou shared wisdom during an Oprah Master's Class. Reflect on the transcript of that video:

> There is an African American song—nineteenth
> century—which is so great, and it says (she starts
> to sing), "When it looks like the sun will not shine
> anymore, God put a rainbow in the clouds." (she
> stops singing) Imagine, and I have had so many
> rainbows in my clouds, I have had a lot of clouds, but
> I have had so many rainbows, and one of the things
> I do when I step up on the stage, when I stand up
> to translate, when I go to teach my classes, when I
> go to direct a movie, I bring everyone who has ever
> been kind to me (pause) Black, white, Asian, Native
> American, gay, straight, everybody. I say, "Come
> with me, we are going on the stage; come with me
> I need you now." They all did, you see, so I don't
> ever feel I have no help. I've had rainbows in my
> clouds, and the thing to do it seems to me (pause)
> is to prepare yourself so that you can be a rainbow

in somebody else's cloud. Somebody who may not look like you, may not call God the same name you call God, if they call God at all you see. They may not eat the same dishes prepared the way you do, may not dance your dances, or speak your language, but be a blessing to somebody. That's what I think.

Maya Angelou reminds us that we can prepare ourselves to be a rainbow in the clouds. When we lead with love, we elevate our ability to respond purposefully and productively to adversity. We all know that rainbows ignite hope, and love nourishes and engages us in living and learning with intention.

 CORE CONNECTION

Ownership is our ability to take responsibility for our responses and actions. It requires that we avoid blaming others or outside factors for the challenges. Instead, we focus on the steps we can take to improve the situations, resulting in greater self-efficacy and the recognition that our efforts and the outcomes are connected (Stoltz, 1997).

To lead with love is to own our role, not only as Ignitors of Hope, but as leaders of our own lives. Leading with love helps us to respond to adverse conditions from a place of self-reflection, compassion, and acceptance. When we lead with love, we acknowledge the import of modeling skills and behaviors that demonstrate self-efficacy, accountability, and solution-seeking. Finally, teaching ownership through the lens of love provides opportunities for our students to practice agency and for our staff to invest in creating a Community of Care to support one another in the face of adversity, enhance the well-being of staff and students alike, and ignite hope for all!

FINAL REFLECTION

In the introduction of this book, we asked you to consider the prayer for serenity by Reinhold Niebuhr:

*Grant me the serenity to accept
the things I cannot change,*

the courage to change the things I can,

and the wisdom to know the difference.

We also suggested that encountering adversity is central to the human experience. It is our hope that throughout each lesson, you were able to contemplate the way in which you respond to significant adversity. We thank you for exploring the ideas, practices, and strategies we shared. We ask that you challenge yourself to identify your own strengths that may have come to light throughout your reading of this book and that you recognize all the ways in which you already ignite hope, nourish well-being, and engage students. Then, contemplate new content gained from your reading. We ask that you look back at the serenity prayer and replace the words "the things" with specific words or terms applicable to your practice or your life experiences. In doing so, perhaps the process of visualizing each line with words or terms specific to you or your needs may actually catalyze your ability to find the serenity to accept, the courage to change, and the wisdom to know the difference.

We began our journey with you with specific goals. As a result, we hope that you have gained strategies for nourishing your well-being and that of your students. We expect having arrived at this final reflection that you are more aware of the situations in your life, personally and at work, that are out of your control and those for which you have agency and can take meaningful action through your thoughts, words, and behaviors. We have confidence that you have skills that you learned within the lessons of this book to cultivate courage to pursue intentional change. We hope to have empowered you with strategies to foster your students' abilities to effectively respond to adversity.

Finally, we suggested in the introduction the value of the concept *all teach, all learn*. In the Appendix, we have provided a list of additional activities and strategies specific to the role you serve within your school community and categorized into the lessons we included in this book. Consider each of the activities or strategies through the lens of your vocational role. Reflect on what might work for you and your students and what is not applicable and why. Tweak ideas or modify suggested activities and strategies to make them your own. Be assured that you possess the skills and ability to elevate your adversity quotient and support your students in doing the same.

Thank you for taking time to reflect on the activities and strategies specific to your vocational role. We ask that, as you turn the last page, you consider this moment as a beginning rather than an end. We hope you are empowered with tools to invest in teaching and learning in the face of adversity and that you feel a rekindled sense of purpose and a renewed spirit. Remember, you chose this vocation for a reason. As you step into school each day, know that you possess the ability to elevate your adversity quotient and the capacity to support your students with instructional practices, strategies, and resources to assist them in responding effectively to the adversity in their lives.

In closing, let us tell you about Frankie Benitez. By the age of 14, Frankie was no longer interested in school. For most of his life, he had experienced what he felt to be insurmountable obstacles. His home life was volatile. Alcoholism and domestic violence seemed to collide regularly. It was no wonder that Frankie came to school looking for fights himself. Frankie was constantly reeling from the loss of loved ones and good friends because of the lifestyle they led. Frankie never knew how to balance the strong emotions he felt with his responsibilities at home to help his mother to care for his younger siblings and the demands of school, which he admitted seemed senseless. He used alcohol in excess as an escape and identified more with the language of gangs than the language of school. Perhaps he felt disconnected from school because by the ninth grade he still struggled to read. When challenges occurred for Frankie, he often threw up his hands and said, "Who cares?" or "I can't, so why even try!" Frankie's adversity quotient was low. His belief in himself and his ability to respond to challenges in a way that helped his situation was void of hope. By the end of ninth grade, a combination of Frankie's truancy, fighting, alcohol abuse, and lack of credits resulted in him being sent to an alternative school.

Frankie, age 16

Source: Frankie Benitez. Used with permission.

This school was uniquely designed to provide students with a second chance. Every staff member was committed to seeking to understand their students, to meet them in the moment, and to focus on what each student could achieve based on their strengths. They provided opportunities for Frankie to realize that the choices he made influenced his future. Thus, Frankie came to perceive that he had control over his life, and his adversity quotient began to rise. As a result, Frankie slowing began taking responsibility for his part in the conflict at home and his lack of achievement at school. In doing so, he noticed that he had tools to respond to the adversity that typically seemed to reach into all aspects of his life. He had adults in his life who believed in him. He made meaningful connections at school with adults and students, and he began to feel valued and willing to engage in his own learning (including reading!) and invest in his school community. Frankie learned how to set goals, develop agency, and be accountable, and these skills transferred into Frankie's adulthood.

Frankie is now a committed husband, a loving father of three children, and a reliable leader within a successful company. He is a human being who gives back to his community. Frankie has been known to reach out regularly to the staff from his alternative school to express gratitude and check in.

Frankie and his family

Source: Frankie Benitez. Used with permission.

Today, Frankie still encounters adversity, yet he is able to respond to obstacles, uncertainty, and substantial challenges with fortitude, strategies, and tangible hope. He credits the adults at his school as his "why"—his reason for being a person he never imagined he could be. These adults are educators just like you! You have undoubtedly encountered "Frankies" in your life. Never doubt your ability to make a difference in the life of a child who is up against all odds. Know that your efforts will make a difference in life too!

Be assured that when you work *with* your colleagues to believe in your students and your impact on their learning—when you think, speak, and act with intention—when you lead from a place of love, seeking to understand your students and their families—you ignite hope! Furthermore, when you make a conscientious effort to connect intentionally and put specific instructional and restorative practices into action, you not only nourish your own well-being but you support the well-being of others. Finally, when you remember and renew why you do what you do and when you set relevant goals for yourself and encourage your students to do the same, you, your colleagues, and your students will realize the value of teaching and learning in the face of adversity!

In closing, with hope in our hearts, we want you to know how much we appreciate you, your experiences with adversity, and your commitment to your school community.

APPENDIX

Activities That Ignite
Hope, Nourish Well-Being,
and Engage Students

ACTIVITY ONE: BE INTENTIONAL

ALL STAFF

Write down the story of your why. Share it with someone you trust and/or share your why with at least one student per week.

~~~

Ask at least one student per week why they believe school is important.

~~~

Ask students to share one ambition they have for their future. Follow up by asking if they have a plan to step toward that ambition.

~~~

Make a statement of gratitude each morning as you greet yourself in the mirror. If this doesn't seem natural to you, write a few words of encouragement or gratitude on a Post-it™ note and place it on your mirror so that it is the first thing you see each morning. Periodically, update.

~~~

Greet colleagues, students, and students' family members by name. If you don't know someone's name, introduce yourself and ask for their name as well.

If you have difficulty remembering names, associate an adjective starting with the same letter of the person's first name to help you to remember. For example, you might say to yourself: Auburn Analese or Mighty Malik.

~~~

Make eye contact, when appropriate. Note that among some peoples, averting eyes is a sign of respect.

~~~

Stop, look, ask, and listen. If you ask someone how they are, stop to look into their eyes as you listen to their answer. Never ask in passing or as a greeting. It implies that you aren't truly interested in the answer. If you don't have time to stop, then change the question to a statement, such as, "Good morning. I hope you have a wonderful day!"

~~~

Take one intentional breath when you're feeling overwhelmed, frustrated, or anxious. Slowly breathe in through your nose, hold the breath for a few seconds, and then slowly breathe out through your mouth. This small step can help you to center yourself, refocus, or reframe your thoughts, words, or behaviors.

EDUCATIONAL LEADERS

Talk about your why. Share with your staff and discuss the value of renewing one's why.

~~~

Provide opportunities for your staff to share their why.

1. Ask them to reflect and journal the reason or reasons they originally chose to pursue their vocational career.

2. Offer a Stand/Sit challenge. For example, stand if you know your why without question; stay seated if you need time to think about it. Ask staff to join small groups, including at least one who stood and one who remained seated. In small groups, ask those who stood to share.

The task for those who remained seated is to choose one person with whom to share on a specific date and time after they have had time to reflect. The chosen person is accountable for checking in to ensure the discussion occurs.

3. During a staff meeting, engage in a "Why Do You Do?" activity. This is an activity in which participants pair and share based on the following hypothetical scenario: You are at a dinner party and don't know the person seated across the table from you. Please introduce yourselves, and rather than asking the typical question of "What do you do?" instead ask, "Why do you do?" It may help to provide an example of the difference between the two.

Typical

Partner 1: "Hello, my name is Tameka."

Partner 2: "Hi, my name is Raul."

Partner 1: "Nice to meet you. So, Raul, what do you do?"

Partner 2: "I'm a high school principal. What do you do?"

Versus

Partner 1: "Hello, my name is Tameka."

Partner 2: "Hi, my name is Raul."

Partner 1: "Nice to meet you, Raul. So, Raul, *why* do you do what you do?"

Partner 2: "I know that many students struggle with school. I serve as a principal at an alternative education high school because I can create opportunities for my students to feel accepted and experience a fresh start while coming to believe in themselves and their ability to learn."

~~~

Initiate a WHY TRY Family Night. Note that the goal is to encourage a focus on finding purpose and meaning in learning and living.

Provide each family with a poster board to create an answer to the question WHY TRY. They can write inspirational quotes, draw pictures, or share brief testimony in written form. After review, place these posters around the school. Variations of this activity can include stations in which specific prompts are discussed. Prompts can include questions such as WHY TRY math? Or WHY TRY to learn something new every day? It can be fun to have each class or grade level come up with a different prompt.

~~~

Be available at the school entrance before school to welcome students each day. Let them see you at the end of the day as you wish them well until you see them again tomorrow.

~~~

Follow through. If you set an expectation for staff or students, check in to make sure that the expectation is being met or to inquire if the individual needs support to meet the expectation.

~~~

Create a shared-staff electronic form to recognize the strengths of staff members. Delegate recognition efforts equally among your administrative team so that every staff member is recognized within a predetermined amount of time. Provide a comments section to allow other staff members to contribute to the recognition.

~~~

Make at least three positive family phone calls per week to recognize a student. Focus on a strength, positive behavior, or recognized act of kindness. Or send at least three positive postcards home each week. Attempt to personalize in two sentences or less.

~~~

Provide opportunities for staff to discuss why they, as a group, believe in their students' ability to achieve and why it is imperative that they, as a group, believe in the impact they can have on student achievement. Connect back to research on collective teacher efficacy's influence on student learning.

TEACHERS

If knowing *our* why helps us to find meaning and purpose in all that we do, the same is true for our students. Provide opportunities for them to talk with each other about why education is important.

Challenge students to work together to create a list of reasons why caring about their education is beneficial to their future.

~~~

Share the stories or testimonies of celebrities, athletes, and everyday heroes with whom students might identify— those that depict the importance of living a meaningful or purpose-oriented life.

~~~

Ask students to connect different aspects of learning to a current need or future goal.

~~~

Ask students to create a model with clay or another artistic medium that represents a visual representation of why learning is important, where commitment to education will lead, or what meaningful living might look like.

~~~

Model self-awareness. Obviously, there is no need to share one's life story or innermost feelings with our students. However, there is an opportunity for modeling healthy social-emotional well-being by letting students know if you are having a rough morning and need to take a moment to breathe. In fact, invite them to breathe with you.

~~~

Embrace clarity. Choose your words carefully, remembering that less can be more.

~~~

Take an intentional breath when frustrated by a student's inappropriate behavior. Then, address the student privately, as opposed to doing so in front of the class.

1. Consider your body language, keeping your stance open, hands open, and your arms at your sides.

2. Begin with a positive statement.

~~~

Verbally acknowledge that you believe in your students and tell them *why* you believe in them by indicating a specific strength they possess.

~~~

Note: Sometimes it is necessary to consider a negative or disruptive behavior and reframe it as a strength. For example, if a student is always interrupting or out of their desk, help that student to recognize that perseverance is a strength, and they possess it!

~~~

Considering the activities, ideas, and strategies just listed, please choose one or two on which to focus as you respond to the following prompts.

1. I already do this! This is what it looks like in my vocational practice:

_____

_____

_____

_____

_____

_____

_____

_____

2. I would like to try this. This is what it could look like in my vocational practice:

_____

_____

_____

_____

_____

_____

_____

_____

_____

ACTIVITY TWO: CREATE CONNECTIONS

ALL STAFF

Reflect upon the connections you have made within your school community. Ask yourself if there are any opportunities to grow within your relationships with your colleagues, students, or your students' families. If so, choose one relationship on which to focus.

~~~

Consider your reflections from this section regarding ways in which you have lived your life with your hands, eyes, heart, and mind open. Take it a step further by identifying an area of your life in which you have been close-minded or -hearted. Create a personal challenge or action plan to expand your thinking or modify your behavior in this specific area.

~~~

Choose one student or colleague whom you don't know well and spend a few minutes per day intentionally in their presence. There needn't be specific questions asked or activities planned—just time spent.

EDUCATIONAL LEADERS

Foster emotional and social connections.

1. Make time for fun. Consider beginning staff meetings with a check-in circle using "would you rather" questions or one-word prompts. For example, would you rather, forever more, have feathers for skin or scales? Or, what is one word that represents something/someone who brings you joy?

2. Celebrate staff accomplishments and strengths, individually and collectively.

3. Reach out to families through phone calls and letter writing. Recognize their child's strengths or invite involvement in the school community.

~~~

Be restorative in building your school community.

1. Provide opportunities to build trust within your staff body. Work trust-building and team-building activities into routine staff meetings.

2. Create opportunities for staff to laugh together by playing games, sharing fun stories and experiences, or telling appropriate jokes.

3. Create opportunities to build trust within your student body by recognizing and celebrating student strengths and accomplishments, communicating with families, and building time into your weekly or monthly schedule to participate in an all-school activity. (We tend to be so focused on academic instruction that we forget that time spent building connections will transfer to authentic investment in school, including academics.)

~~~

Be restorative in your discipline practices.

Set high expectations and firm boundaries. If an offense occurs, begin by asking affective questions such as these:

a. Can you tell me more about what happened?

b. What were you thinking at the time?

c. What have you thought about since this happened?

d. How did this situation impact or affect you?

e. How do you think it impacted or affected others?

f. What do you think needs to happen to make this situation right?

g. If consequences are necessary, ensure that they are meaningful and connected to the offense.

TEACHERS

Create opportunities to build trust within your classroom community.

1. Greet students by name every day.

2. Maintain a check-in routine or morning meeting routine.

3. Celebrate student successes.

4. Solution-seek in pairs, small groups, or as a class. Share solutions and recognize opportunities to grow.

5. Honor failure as an opportunity to learn. Use yourself or relevant role models as an example.

~~~

Create opportunities for students to work together in random groups, being cognizant to use a variety of different routines for grouping.

Provide opportunities for students to practice agency. If necessary, provide limited choices so that even though guided by you, students are still able to choose their preference. Choice often leads to genuine investment in the task and cooperation among students.

~~~

Understand, practice, and model social-emotional well-being skills. Explicitly teach social-emotional learning skills to your students and integrate them into your lessons.

~~~

Access online resources such as those listed here to expand the activities, strategies, and integration plans available to you in the realm of creating connections, relationship-building, and trust-building:

➤ casel.org

➤ harmonysel.org

➤ pureedgeinc.org

~~~

Considering the activities, ideas, and strategies just listed, please choose a one or two on which to focus as you respond to the following prompts.

1. I already do this! This is what it looks like in my vocational practice:

_____

_____

_____

_____

_____

_____

_____

_____

_____

_____

2. I would like to try this. This is what it could look like in my vocational practice:

_____

_____

_____

_____

_____

_____

_____

_____

ACTIVITY THREE: SEEK TO UNDERSTAND

ALL STAFF

Practice authentic curiosity. Ask yourself, How well do I know my colleagues, the students, and the students' families at my school? Considerations: Do you know where they live? Do you know their interests outside of school? Do you know what their concerns are for work or school?

~~~

Initiate a conversation with a colleague or student, beginning with, "Would you mind telling me more about . . ."

. . . your family

. . . your interests outside of school

. . . your family customs or traditions

. . . something you enjoy about school/work

. . . something that challenges you at school/work

~~~

Consider your understanding and/or knowledge of historical, societal, and systemic racism. Based on your level of understanding, you might choose to expand your knowledge:

1. Read books written by people who have personally experienced racism:

    Ibram X. Kendi: *How to Be an Antiracist* and *Four Hundred Souls: A Community History of African America, 1619–2019*

    Ijeoma Oluo: *So You Want to Talk About Race*

Beverly Daniel Tatum: *Why Are All the Black Kids Sitting Together in the Cafeteria?*

Dena Simmons: *White Rules for Black People*

2. Research social justice; racial justice; culturally relevant instruction; and race, class, and/or gender conflict theory.

3. Examine implicit biases. There are a variety of implicit bias assessments, such as the Harvard Implicit Project, that can be taken online, reflected upon, and discussed.

~~~

If in conflict with or irritated by (yes, we all get irritated on occasion!) a colleague, student, or school community member, listen to understand.

Hold your body in an open stance, keeping your hands at your sides, palms open, feet at least shoulder-width apart with one foot back farther than the other (sometimes when conflict occurs, people feel trapped or unsafe . . . an open stance promotes safety and trust).

EDUCATIONAL LEADERS

Review your data to identify racial, socioeconomic, and special education disparities. Look for disproportionality based on ethnicity, poverty, or ability in the realm of discipline, suspension, and expulsion; participation in gifted programs or advanced placement classes; free and reduced meal participation; attendance; and so on. Share your findings with your staff and seek solutions as a collective body to reduce such disparities.

~~~

Provide opportunities for your staff to learn from each other. First, create agreements for respectful, brave conversations. Carve out time for dialogue. Choose a courageous topic that impacts your school community, such as racism, poverty, accessibility, or gender identity, and ask questions such as these:

1. How do you experience what is happening (regarding the topic)?

2. How is bias or discrimination evident in our school community?

3. What have you witnessed?

4. What questions do you have?

5. Is there anything you are concerned or confused about?

6. How might we better support each other, our students, or our families?

7. How might we combat discrimination or bias within our school community?

~~~

Create family traditions or a culture night in which families can set up a station to share their customs or traditions through crafts, foods, or activities.

TEACHERS

As a writing assignment, ask students to share three things they would like you to know about them that would help you to know them and support them throughout the school year. This is important to do at the beginning of the school year but should be repeated throughout the year, as students' lived experiences may alter their needs.

~~~

Provide opportunities for students to share with and learn about each other. For example, the Inside/Outside Cup or

Brown Bag Activity helps students to learn to appreciate each other for who they are on the inside versus what is assumed or perceived based on appearance, performance, or behavior. The activity typically requires each student to decorate a paper or Styrofoam cup or a brown bag. On the outside, the student decorates with words or symbols that represent what people "see" and therefore assume. How the student looks, what they are involved in, the attitude they present publicly, or other outward traits may be included. On the inside, the student might include words or symbols that represent family, feelings, character, or personality traits that aren't obvious or known by most people and lived experiences of which most people aren't aware. As a teacher, you may dedicate a class period for sharing or have a few students share per week. Be sure to set agreements for sharing and discussion that promote respect and appreciation for diversity.

~~~

Read or discuss topics with your students that honor diversity, promote social or racial justice, or address educational or societal inequities.

~~~

Be aware of students' individual needs based on culture or ability. For example, if eye contact is uncomfortable or inappropriate for a student, sit or stand beside them while interacting one on one rather than facing them directly.

~~~

Considering the activities, ideas, and strategies just listed, please choose one or two on which to focus as you respond to the following prompts.

1. I already do this! This is what it looks like in my vocational practice:

_____

_____

_____

_____

_____

_____

_____

_____

_____

2. I would like to try this. This is what it could look like in my vocational practice:

_____

_____

_____

_____

_____

_____

_____

_____

_____

_____

ACTIVITY FOUR: LEAD WITH LOVE

ALL STAFF

When experiencing feelings related to a person or situation, ask yourself, Are these feelings coming from a place of love or a place of fear?

~~~

Consider the way in which you demonstrate a loving attitude toward your colleagues, students, and students' families.

~~~

Each month, write down one strength and one opportunity for growth in this regard as a celebration and challenge or professional goal.

~~~

Once a week, practice one random act of kindness. Keep it anonymous if possible. You will notice that what may take planning initially will become spontaneous and instinctive as you continue to practice.

EDUCATIONAL LEADERS

Talk about love . . . love of humanity, education, vocation, and experiences.

~~~

Provide opportunities for staff to discuss what love "looks like" in the realm of your school community. Does or can it look like kindness, respect, compassion, empathy, honoring diversity, acceptance, cooperation, collaboration, service, or _____?

~~~

Model "love" as an action word. Show by your example that you are making a concerted effort to act and respond from a place of love in your words, attitudes, and behaviors.

~~~

Create a "Share the Love" electronic document in which students, staff, and/or school community members can contribute comments of appreciation for one another. From this document, people can be recognized and celebrated.

TEACHERS

Create opportunities for students to recognize love as an action. Show video clips demonstrating kindness, empathy, or acts of compassion.

~~~

Create opportunities for students to participate in random acts of kindness or appreciation for others. For example, ask students to choose a person in their family, neighborhood, or school community to whom they will write an appreciation note. Provide an opportunity to write and create a plan for distribution.

~~~

Model love through listening, seeking to understand, and demonstrating respect.

~~~

Considering the activities, ideas, and strategies just listed, please choose one or two on which to focus as you respond to the following prompts.

1. I already do this! This is what it looks like in my vocational practice:

_____

_____

_____

_____

_____

_____

_____

_____

_____

2. I would like to try this. This is what it could look like in my
   vocational practice:

_____

_____

_____

_____

_____

_____

_____

_____

_____

_____

REFERENCES

Acosta, J., Chinman, M., Ebener, P., Malone, P. S., Phillips, A., & Wilks, A. (2019). Evaluation of a whole-school change intervention: Findings from a two-year cluster-randomized trial of the restorative practices intervention. *Journal of Youth & Adolescence, 48*(5), 876-890.

Bandura, A. (1982). Self-efficacy mechanism in human agency. *American Psychologist, 37*(2), 122-147.

Bandura, A., & Locke, E. A. (2003). Negative self-efficacy and goal effects revisited. *Journal of Applied Psychology, 88*(1), 87-99. doi: 10.1037/0021-9010.88.1.87

Birch, S. H., & Ladd, G. W. (1997) The teacher-child relationship and children's early school adjustment. *Journal of School Psychology, 35*, 61-79. http://dx.doi.org/10.1016/S0022-4405(96)00029-5

Bryce, C. I., Alexander, B. L., Fraser, A. M., & Fabes, R. A. (2019). Dimensions of hope in adolescence: Relations to academic functioning and well-being. *Psychology in Schools*. doi/epdf/10.1002/pits.22311

Carter, E. W. (2021). Dimensions of belonging for individuals with intellectual and developmental disabilities. In J. L. Jones & K. L. Gallus (Eds.), *Belonging and resilience in individuals with developmental disabilities* (pp. 13-33). Springer Nature.

Chamorro-Premuzic, T., & Lusk, D. (2017, August 16). The dark side of resilience. *Harvard Business Review*. https://hbr.org/2017/08/the-dark-side-of-resilience#:~:text=In%20sum%2C%20there%20is%20no,of%20unpleasant%20or%20counterproductive%20circumstances

Cohen, G. L. (2022). *Belonging: The science of creating connection and bridging divides*. W. W. Norton & Co.

Cornelius-White, J. (2007). Learner-centered teacher-student relationships are effective: A meta-analysis. *Review of Educational Research, 77*(1), 113-143.

Day, L., Hanson, K., Maltby, J., Proctor, C., & Wood, A. (2010). Hope uniquely predicts objective academic achievement above intelligence, personality, and previous academic achievement. *Journal of Research in Personality, 44,* 550-553.

Dennison, K. (2022, June 17). Using intelligence quotients creatively can help you build a dynamic team. *Forbes Magazine.* https://www.forbes.com/sites/karadennison/2022/06/17/using-intelligence-quotients-creatively-can-help-you-build-a-dynamic-team/?sh=7f871e501983

Filippello, P., Buzzai, C., Costa, S., Orecchio, S., & Sorrenti, L. (2020). Teaching style and academic achievement: The mediating role of learned helplessness and mastery orientation. *Psychology in the Schools, 57*(1), 5-16. https://doi.org/10.1002/pits.22315

Goddard, R. D., Hoy, W. K., & Woolfolk Hoy, A. (2004). Collective efficacy beliefs: Theoretical developments, empirical evidence, and future directions. *Educational Researcher, 33*(3), 3-13.

Good, T. (1987). Two decades of research on teacher expectations. *Journal of Teacher Education, 38*(4), 32-47.

Gordon, N. (2018, January 18). *Disproportionality in student discipline: Connecting policy to research.* Brookings. https://www.brookings.edu/research/disproportionality-in-student-discipline-connecting-policy-to-research/

Hall, R. M., & Sandler, B. R. (1982). *The classroom climate: A chilly one for women?* Project on the Status of Women. https://files.eric.ed.gov/fulltext/ED215628.pdf

Hamre, B. K., & Pianta, R. C. (2010). Classroom environments and developmental processes. In J. L. Meece & J. S. Eccles (Eds.), *Handbook of research on schools, schooling, and human development* (pp. 25-41). Routledge.

Hendrickx, M. M. H. G., Mainhard, T., Oudman, S., Boor-Klip, H. J., & Brekelmans, M. (2017). Teacher behavior and peer liking and disliking: The teacher as a social referent for peer status. *Journal of Educational Psychology, 109*(4), 546-558.

Jensen, E. (2009). *Teaching with poverty in mind: What being poor does to kids' brains and what schools can do about it.* ASCD.

Jensen, E. (2019, April 22). 5 takeaways on vulnerability from Brené Brown's "The call to courage." *USA TODAY.* https://www.usatoday.com/story/life/tv/2019/04/19/brene-brown-call-courage-netflix-vulnerability/3497969002/

Jordan, H. (2023, October 19). Why school discipline reform still matters. *American Civil Liberties Union.* www.aclu.org/news/racial-justice/why-school-discipline-reform-still-matters

Killingsworth, M. A., & Gilbert, D. T. (2010, November 12). A wandering mind is an unhappy mind. *Science.* https://science.sciencemag.org/content/330/6006/932.abstract

Locke, E., & Latham, G. (1991). A theory of goal setting & task performance. *The Academy of Management Review, 16.* 10.2307/258875

MIT Teaching + Learning Lab. (n.d.). *Students' sense of belonging matters: Evidence from three studies.* https://tll.mit.edu/sense-of-belonging-matters/

Naglieri, J. A. (2020). *Thinking versus knowing: The key to measuring intelligence.* National Association of School Psychologists. https://www.nasponline.org/professional-development/a-closer-look-blog/thinking-versus-knowing-the-key-to-measuring-intelligence

National Research Council. (2012). *Education for life and work: Developing transferable knowledge and skills in the 21st century.* The National Academies Press.

National Scientific Council on the Developing Child. (2015). *Supportive relationships and active skill-building strengthen the foundations of resilience: Working Paper 13.* http://www.developingchild.harvard.edu

Nese, R. N. T., Nese, J. F. T., McCroskey, C., Meng, P., Triplett, D., & Bastable, E. (2021). Moving away from disproportionate exclusionary discipline: Developing and utilizing a continuum of preventative and instructional supports. *Preventing School Failure, 65*(2), 1-11.

Nese, R. N. T., Santiago-Rosario, M. R., Malose, S., Hamilton, J., Nese, J. F. T., & Horner, R. (2022). Improving a universal intervention for reducing exclusionary discipline practices using student and teacher guidance. *Psychology in the Schools, 59,* 2042-2061. https://doi.org/10.1002/pits.22576

Norton Hamre, B. K., Pianta, R. C., Downer, J. T., DeCoster, J., Mashburn, A. J., Jones, S. M., Brown, J. L., Cappella, E., Atkins, M., Rivers, S. E., Brackett, M. A., & Hamagami, A. (2013). Teaching through interactions. *Elementary School Journal, 113*(4), 461-487. [update from Hamre and Pianta, 2005]

Obama, M. (2011, June 22). *Remarks by the First Lady during keynote address at young African women leaders forum.* Whitehouse.gov .obamawhitehouse.archives.gov/the-press-office/2011/06/22/ remarks-first-lady-during-keynote-address-young-african-wom en-leaders-fo

Office for Civil Rights. (2023, November). *2020-21 civil rights data collection student discipline and school climate in U.S. public schools.* https://www2.ed.gov/about/offices/list/ocr/docs/ crdc-discipline-school-climate-report.pdf

Osher, D., Cantor, P., Berg, J., Steyer, L., & Rose, T. (2020) Drivers of human development: How relationships and context shape learning and development. *Applied Developmental Science, 24*(1), 6-36. https://doi.org/10.1002/pits.22576

Peña, P. A., & Duckworth, A. L. (2018). The effects of relative and absolute age in the measurement of grit from 9th to 12th grade. *Economics of Education Review, 66,* 183-190. https://doi .org/10.1016/j.econedurev.2018.08.009

Pintrich, P. R. (2003). A motivational science perspective on the role of student motivation in learning and teaching contexts. *Journal of Educational Psychology, 95,* 667-686.

Pipas, C. F., & Pepper, E. L. (2021). Building community well-being through emotional intelligence and cognitive reframing. *Family Practice Management, 28*(1), 23-26.

Ratner, P. (2019, January 30). Scientists find out how hope protects the brain. *Big Think.* bigthink.com/hope-optimism/ scientists-find-out-how-hope-protects-the-brain

Samuel, S. (2020, June 29). *Why Cornel West is hopeful (but not optimistic).* Vox. https://www.vox.com/future-perfect/ 2020/7/29/21340730/cornel-west-coronavirus-racism-way- through-podcast

Shepherd, S., Owen, D., & Fitch, T. J. (2006). Locus of control and academic achievement in high school students. *Psychological Reports, 98*(2), 318-322. https://doi.org/10.2466/ PR0.98.2.318-322

Stanovich, K. E. (1986). Matthew effects in reading: Some consequences of individual differences in the acquisition of literacy. *Reading Research Quarterly, 22,* 360-407.

Stoltz, P. (1997). *Adversity quotient: Turning obstacles into opportunities.* Wiley.

Terman, L. M. (1916). *The measurement of intelligence: An explanation of and a complete guide for the use of the Standard revision and extension of the Binet-Simon intelligence scale.* Houghton Mifflin.

Wachtel, T. (2016). *Defining restorative.* IIRP graduate school. https://www.iirp.edu/images/pdf/Defining-Restorative_Nov-2016.pdf

Watson, S. (2023, June 13). *Oxytocin: The love hormone.* Harvard Health. https://www.health.harvard.edu/mind-and-mood/oxytocin-the-love-hormone

West, C. [@CornelWest]. (2013, December 5). You can't lead the people if you don't love the people. You can't save the people if you don't serve the people. [Tweet]. Twitter. https://twitter.com/CornelWest/status/408819728770027521

Wisconsin Department of Public Instruction. (n.d.). *Wisconsin's guiding principles for teaching and learning.* https://dpi.wi.gov/standards/guiding-principles

Xing, L., Deng, S. W., & Ho, G. W. (2023). From empathy to resilience: The mediating role of emotional intelligence. *Psychological Reports.* https://doi.org/10.1177/00332941231220299.

Zeiser, K., Scholz, C., & Cirks, V. (2018). *Maximizing student agency: Implementing and measuring student-centered learning practices.* American Institutes of Research. https://files.eric.ed.gov/fulltext/ED592084.pdf

INDEX

Keep learning...

More from Michelle Trujillo

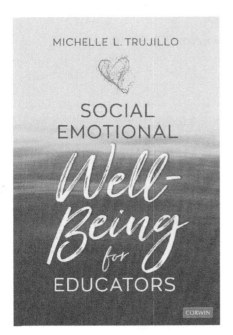

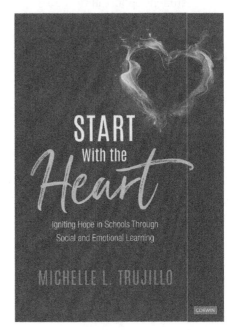

A Sage Company

Helping educators make the greatest impact

CORWIN HAS ONE MISSION: to enhance education through intentional professional learning.

We build long-term relationships with our authors, educators, clients, and associations who partner with us to develop and continuously improve the best evidence-based practices that establish and support lifelong learning.

Made in the USA
Middletown, DE
08 January 2025

69116977R00097